Douglas M.

With One Accord

AFFIRMING CATHOLIC TEACHING USING PROTESTANT PRINCIPLES

Catholic Answers Press

Published by Catholic Answers, Inc.
2020 Gillespie Way
El Cajon, California 92020
1-888-291-8000 orders
619-387-0042 fax
catholic.com

Printed in the United States of America

Cover by Theodore Schluenderfritz
Interior by Russell Graphic Design

978-1-68357-189-6
978-1-68357-190-2 Kindle
978-1-68357-191-9 ePub

I want to thank my wife for her bravery and faithfulness, and my kids, who are growing into such amazing people despite the fact that daddy seems to spend a lot of time reading, my mother for her encouragement, trust, and editing, and my dad for always bragging on me. I cannot individually thank all those who took the time to help guide me through the thicket of Catholic-Protestant debates, but I must express gratitude to Scott Hahn, Jason Reed, and especially Devin Rose who stood by me through every step (whether forward or backward). Finally, I want to express heartfelt thanks to the team at Catholic Answers—especially my editor, Todd Aglialoro, for his skill and willingness to work with me on this book.

CONTENTS

INTRO

Principles and Particulars.....................7

1

Church and Authority.......................... 15

2

Scripture and Tradition 33

3

Worship and Sacraments..................... 61

4

Mary and the Saints 95

5

Sin and Morality 115

6

Salvation and Purgatory.....................129

POSTSCRIPT

Unity and Division............................159

Principles and Particulars

To outsiders, Catholicism is weird.

Protestants, especially, often have a hard time comprehending the Catholic world of popes, Mary statues, prayer cards, vestments, smells, bells, and Jesus' actual body and blood in the Eucharist—especially if they have been taught that these are unbiblical additions to the pure Christian faith.

Of course, all of Christianity can seem pretty weird, can't it?

All Christians believe in a God that is one yet somehow also three. We think that a man who is also God died to bring life to those who are spiritually dead. We think that a snake talked a couple into eating a piece of fruit that ruined the world. We believe in talking donkeys.

In light of this, it seems that the perceived weirdness of Catholic Christianity may not be a very good reason for Protestant Christians to reject it. If weirdness is a good reason to reject Catholicism, it is just as good a reason to reject

Christianity entirely. Further, Protestantism has its own examples of weirdness, ranging from sweating television evangelists and arena-rock worship to "drunk in the spirit" congregants flopping around on the church floor or handling poisonous snakes to prove they are Spirit-filled.

No, most Protestants will say that it's not Catholic weirdness alone that causes them to reject the Church—it's disagreements over Catholic doctrines that they consider incompatible with Christianity. I wrote this book to explore some of those key disagreements in the hope of overcoming them, or at least shrinking the distance they cover.

The Bible tells us that, after Christ's ascension but before the descent of the Holy Spirit, his followers gathered in the upper room, where they devoted themselves to worship "with one accord" (Acts 1:14). These earliest Christians were marked by *unity of faith*—a unity that, however splintered today, is still our goal (cf. John 17:21). And I think many Protestants may be closer to it than they think.

Why? Because lots of the weird Christian principles they believe *actually set up nicely for arriving at Catholic particulars.* Maybe they don't see it because they haven't connected the dots, or because of historical bias, or because of some small logical or exegetical obstacle, or simply because no one has explained one key piece of information to them. But the dots can be connected, the bias overcome, the correct logic and info supplied.

In these pages, that's what I hope to do: show how, on so many of the matters of Catholic belief that Protestants think they must radically reject, they're actually not very far away from agreement. In fact, what they already believe as Protestants is a foundation for agreement with the Catholic position. At least that's what I discovered on my journey. When it comes to the Eucharist, Mary and the saints,

Scripture and Tradition, and more, we may not be so far away from accord after all.

A Principled Protestant Becomes a Converted Catholic

It's important to mention that I was once a Protestant and am now a Catholic. Some of my family and friends followed me into the Catholic Church, but others didn't, and I still love and respect them very much. I truly and deeply appreciate what I learned and experienced as an Evangelical Protestant, and I continue to value many non-Catholic writers, teachers, and preachers.

I grew up fairly agnostic and did not become a believer in Christianity until college, when I discovered an Evangelical culture that I assumed to be equivalent to Christianity as a whole. Although I had faith in Christ, I had a lot of questions: Why get baptized if I was already "saved"? Why are there three names for one God? What's with the crackers and grape juice? If all predication concerning divinity is necessarily accomplished in terms grounded in the existential knowledge of finite reality, how can they properly be said to signify the unlimited being of God? (Okay, that last one came a lot later.)

I received a lot of conflicting answers to questions like these, and eventually I realized why. Not only were there numerous disagreements among people who all called themselves Christians, there was not just one *thing* called Christianity.

I spent twenty-five years as a committed Evangelical Christian—eventually earning a degree and teaching at an Evangelical seminary for a decade. During that time I got ordained, published, and started speaking across the country. I had arrived. I was "an Evangelical of Evangelicals."[1] But all was not as pleasant as it seemed.

Although I was quite comfortable in my little niche, I began having serious difficulties with Evangelicalism as a whole. Although I had been taught to defend the historic Christian faith, I wasn't sure how to justify such a claim when many of the distinctive doctrines of Evangelicalism hadn't come into existence until the sixteenth through nineteenth centuries. I believed that the Bible was God's word, but I didn't understand how we knew which books belonged in it without trusting the Church that made that determination (the Church we Protestants rejected). Such thoughts gnawed on my mind for several years.[2]

When my questions spurred me to begin investigating Catholicism, I had most of the usual Protestant hang ups: I questioned the infallibility of the pope *(Isn't he just a man?)*, the importance of Mary *(Isn't she just Jesus' mom?)*, the nature of the Eucharist *(How could that piece of bread be Jesus?)*, the role of the Church *(Isn't the Bible enough?)*, and the role of works in salvation *(Isn't it legalism to require them?)*. Added to these were questions about Galileo, the Inquisition, the Crusades, and so on.

Although this list seemed daunting, deeper study found my concerns falling one by one. In some cases they were resolved simply by learning what the Church actually taught or what really happened in history rather than swallowing popular misconceptions or myths. In other cases it took deeper learning, reflection, and prayer.

In my investigation I was moved by good theological reasoning and apologetic arguments, but one of the things that helped me most in my thinking was the numerous parallels that I found between what the Catholic Church taught and what I already believed as a Protestant. These were not usually shared doctrines, of course—otherwise, becoming Catholic would only involve switching churches!

Rather, I discovered several common theological *principles* behind the many divergent doctrinal *particulars*. Once I realized that the same principle can lead to more than one particular, I was able to proceed in a much more gracious and understanding manner.

As I came to see that I already accepted the principle behind many particular Catholic doctrines, I could more quickly cut through to the relevant differences. I realized that if I rejected a particular belief, I either had to abandon the doctrinal principle behind it or show that it was not really equivalent. Sometimes the first option could lead to a rejection of Christianity itself, and the second option was not always easy.

Logical Principles and Particulars

By the terms *principle* and *particular* I am speaking of the distinction between a general truth and the more specific applications of that truth. Arguments often go from principle to particular. In Aristotle's famous logic example, he said that if "all men are mortal" (principle) and "Socrates is a man" (particular) it follows that "Socrates is mortal" (another particular). The trouble is that we rarely speak in such formal logical syllogisms, and for the sake of efficiency in an argument we usually leave out either the principle or the particular and just skip to the conclusion. So, if Aristotle was just walking down the street talking with you, he might simply say, "Socrates is mortal because all men are mortal."

This is not unreasonable—a missing principle or particular in a valid argument can always be deduced from the other parts. This is usually intuitive. For example, if someone says, "You should not smoke because it is unhealthy," it is pretty clear that the unspoken principle is, "You should not do things that are unhealthy." When the particular—"Smoking is unhealthy"— is added to this principle, then the conclusion follows. Of course, many other particulars could flow from the same principle as well (such as, "You should not overeat" or, "You should not play with fire").

Emotions tend to run higher on disagreements over principles than over particulars, which are often less personal, more objective, and easier to discuss. It is often principles, however, that are perceived to be at issue even when it really is just the particulars. In America today, virtually no one would argue that murdering babies should be allowed (as a principle); yet many people think abortion should be legal (as a particular). Until we can properly understand an issue according to its principles and particulars, we will just talk past each other.

From Protestant Premises to Catholic Conclusions?

So, reaching agreement over common principles doesn't always easily lead to agreement on particulars, and this is no less true for differences between Protestants and Catholics. But it's a good place to start. Looking at Catholic-Protestant theological debates on a more principled level can help each side understand the other better, thus avoiding the easy and unhelpful caricatures that often drive such debates. So long as misrepresentation and misinformation cloud the discussion, little progress can be made.

I have a good Protestant friend who enjoys the occasional theological sparring match with me. We have reached a level of friendship where we can really hack on each other with no hurt feelings or misunderstandings—and we take full advantage of this by hurling insults at each other's traditions whenever opportunity arises. Most of our doctrinal debates end with him asking me if I don't have some statues to worship and me asking him which denomination is God's Church this week. We enjoy saying things like this to each other precisely because we both know that they are ridiculous misrepresentations of each other's faith. (Catholic or Protestant, we're still guys!)

Unfortunately, though, many of the silly portrayals of Catholics by Protestants (and Protestants by Catholics) are taken seriously by those who lack a firm grasp of what either side is really about. Of course, if all we know are misrepresentations, we can hardly take the other side seriously. A principled discussion of our differences requires that we cut through the quips and get to the bedrock issues that divide us. Seeing how conflicting particulars can actually be rooted in a common principle can go a long way toward reaching that state, and thus help move the conversation forward instead of miring it in misunderstanding. Sometimes the key to dialogue is not getting someone to see an issue from your perspective—but getting him to see it from his own.

Contentious Contents

In this book, we will begin by looking at the most basic disagreement between Catholics and Protestants—namely, over religious authority. Is it really the case that Catholics simply surrender their minds to the Catholic Church (or the pope) while Protestants retain their intellectual integrity by studying Scripture?

Next, we will look at Scripture and Tradition and see how they relate. Can it be that Catholicism is the product of fallible doctrinal accrual over two millennia while Protestantism retains the pure first-century faith based on the infallible Bible alone?

Following from the Bible and one's interpretive tradition comes worship. Is Christianity a religion or a relationship? Should church services be liturgical or free-roaming? Should we use images? Are our practices mere symbols or do they accomplish something more?

Closely related to our worship of God is the question of veneration. Does Mary have a special place in Christian devotion? Is she an intercessor along with Jesus, her son? Are some prayers merely vain repetition? Do other saints hear our prayers, or is it idolatrous to speak to them at all?

Our day-to-day lives are affected by our faith as well. Is there really a difference between mortal and venial sins, or is it simply that all sin is sin? Are things like divorce and contraception really sinful, or are they merely allowed by God to get us through in this fallen world?

And finally, knowing that we all fall into sin occasionally, what are we to do about it? How is salvation accomplished? Must we add our own works to faith? If Jesus saves us, what is purgatory all about? And how can we be said to merit salvation when it is all from God?

Church and Authority

Early on in my investigation of Catholicism, I realized that of all the various doctrinal, ethical, and practical issues that separate Catholicism from Protestantism, the most important is the Church's view of *authority*. In fact in a sense it is the *only* issue, since once it's settled other issues become secondary.

Many Protestants have some awareness of the issue of authority in religion, but for Catholics it occupies a much more important place. Because most Protestants see their primary authority as the Bible, the authority of any particular church is of negligible importance. From their own reading of Scripture, most Protestants already have some idea of what they believe about Christianity, and so their primary criterion for choosing a church is that it agrees with that understanding. But Catholics do not decide what they believe and then find a particular church that agrees with them; they find the Church that has authority and then let it tell them what to believe. Which way is right?

Bad Bible People

One obstacle to trusting the authority of the Church is that it is made up of imperfect people, and imperfect people make mistakes. It is one thing to trust the authority of an inerrant book inspired by a perfect God. It is quite another to trust the authority of manifestly errant human beings.

Even worse, not only do people often make mistakes—they often do the wrong thing intentionally. The Bible can't sin, but the history of the Church is full of immoral popes, cardinals, bishops, and priests. Given this reality, how could Christians let the Church tell them what to believe?

A biblical example of a similar situation is the nation of Israel. Anyone who knows Old Testament history can tell you that Israel has a pretty checkered past. Nearly every salvation covenant that God made in the Old Testament came with stipulations that Israel failed to honor. Prophets did not always act with virtue, and virtually any sampling from among the nation's kings will turn up some serious vice. Consider several authors of the Old Testament itself:

- Moses, the traditional author of the first five books of the Old Testament, was a murderer who, because of his lack of faith, was not allowed to see the fruit of his ministry to the Hebrews.

- The prophet Jonah was so unwilling to deliver a message that God had commanded him to speak that he and a ship full of sailors were nearly killed.

- King David, who wrote many of the Psalms and who was one of Israel's greatest kings, was also an adulterer and a murderer.

And it wasn't as though Israel's problems were limited to the top of the hierarchy. The common people of Israel also struggled with idolatry and other evils throughout the nation's history.

And yet the people of Israel remained the chosen people of God.

Although many individual Israelites were judged for their heresy or immorality, the nation itself continued to represent God on earth. Israel's kings and prophets did not cease to be legitimate kings and prophets even when they did not do what they were supposed to do. More importantly, when they acted in the roles that God chose them for, their authority was not diminished because of their sinful actions. Jesus seems to acknowledge this in Matthew 23:2–3, and no mainstream Protestant today tries to invalidate Israel's place in salvation history on account of its theological and moral errors.

The Church finds itself in a similar state. God has chosen the Church as his people on earth and established in it a hierarchy of authoritative leadership. He has given this people commands and expectations that have not always been met. However, that does not mean that people holding to authoritative roles in the Church automatically lose those roles when they fail to meet God's expectations. Finally, when those in the Church chosen for specific roles are acting in those roles, they act with authority. This does not mean they will never make mistakes, and that is why there is a hierarchy, but it does mean that they possess religious authority in matters of faith and morals.

IN PRINCIPLE

PROTESTANTS AGREE: God worked in history by granting legitimate religious authority even to imperfect people.

CATHOLICISM AFFIRMS: God grants legitimate religious authority to leaders of the Church even though they are imperfect, sinful people.

The Apostles' Errors

Although some Christians might want to distance themselves from the antics of Old Testament kings, prophets, and other figures, it would be disingenuous to do so with the founders of the Christian faith. Christianity's founder, Jesus Christ, was a perfect example of religious faith, morals, and authority, but those he chose as the foundation stones for his Church were not.

- The brothers James and John, both members of Jesus' apostolic inner circle, argued over who would have top position in the kingdom of God (even to the point of getting their mother involved!).

- The apostle Thomas doubted his associates' report of Jesus' resurrection and famously said that he would not believe it was true unless he could put his fingers in Jesus' wounds.

- The apostle Peter, whom Catholics believe was the primary apostle and the first pope, put his foot in his mouth at nearly every opportunity, and three times denied that he even knew Jesus.

- Jesus even chose Judas, who betrayed his master for thirty pieces of silver and eventually committed suicide over his guilt.

Now, if living an exemplary religious life is a requirement for possessing legitimate religious authority, then we just lost seven books out of the New Testament! If we excluded the apostle Paul for his approval of the murder of the first Christian martyr and his fight against Jesus himself (Acts 9:4), we'd lose another thirteen!

Protestants, who accept the authority of the apostles and of the biblical books they authored, would simply say that God never promised that his people—even his authoritative leaders—would be perfectly good people or would never make mistakes. God simply made sure that, despite their faults, what these men taught about the faith was safeguarded from error (e.g., 1 Cor. 2:13; 2 Pet. 1:20–21). God's grace, not human perfection—that's what is required to make their teachings religiously authoritative.

And that is what the Church teaches about the teaching authority it expresses through its human leaders. Just as Jesus could use imperfect apostles to authoritatively communicate the gospel to the world, he can use imperfect popes, cardinals, and bishops to do the same today.

As we will see next, any Christian who denies that this is how God has operated in the Church is necessarily going to put his faith in serious jeopardy.

IN PRINCIPLE

PROTESTANTS AGREE: The fallible people whom Jesus chose to begin his Church were able, with God's grace, to communicate infallible truths.

IN PARTICULAR

CATHOLICISM AFFIRMS: Fallible Church leaders through the centuries up to today are able, by God's grace, to communicate infallible truths.

A Canon We Can Trust

Because the Bible is inspired by God (as both Catholics and Protestants believe), it is uniquely qualified to serve as our religious authority. The difficulty, though, is that the Bible is not just a book. Rather, it is a collection ("canon") of sacred scriptures—and one without an inspired table of contents.[3] This creates an interesting difficulty for Christians: for if the Bible is taken to be our religious authority, we must be able to identify it![4] So how was the canon of Scripture determined?

Christianity, unlike many other religions, does not have Scripture written or collected by its founder (not directly at least). Instead, the Christian New Testament was written over the course of forty to sixty years by *close followers* of its founder. As Christianity entered its first century of life, these writings had already taken on considerable authority, but so had others. Books like the *Shepherd of Hermas*, the *Didache*, the *Apocalypse of Peter,* and the *Letter of Clement* were also in use by the early Church. Old Testament books were still being debated among the Jews into the first century, and no authoritative New Testament canon existed until the end of fourth.[5]

Notably, the Church did not actually pronounce the complete biblical canon with finality until the sixteenth century, when the Protestant Reformation brought with it questions concerning which books belonged in the Bible. Martin Luther's dislike of the book of James and his skepticism concerning certain "disputed books" in the New Testament is famous, but he was not alone. Ulrich Zwingli also questioned parts of the New Testament canon, and John Calvin wrote of conflicting opinions concerning its various books. Although Catholicism continued to hold to its fourth-century canon, it was not universally defined until the Council of Trent in 1546.

Given the known history of the biblical canon, can we trust that the Church got it right? Some Protestants have expressed fear that to acknowledge the Church's ability to determine the biblical canon is to say that it has authority over the Bible itself. Of course, the Catholic Church makes no claim to have caused the books of the Bible to be inspired;[6] it is a historical fact, though, that the Church assembled the authoritative list of inspired books. Therefore, to put one's faith in the Bible is to trust in the authority of the Church.

To escape this logic, some Protestants have attempted to reverse-engineer the canon so that no religious authority is required to define it. One way to do this is to say that a book can be considered inspired if it is written by one of the apostles of Jesus Christ. We certainly don't need the Church to figure that out, right?

As it turns out, we do—because in many cases it is actually Church tradition that tells us who wrote which books. Not one of the Gospels names its author in the text, the author of the book of Hebrews is anonymous, and there were several men named James in the New Testament who might have been author of the epistle. And then there are several early books that *claim* to be written by an apostle but were not included in the canon of Scripture (e.g., the *Epistle of Barnabas* or the *Apocalypse of St. Peter*). In all of these cases, we must fall back on an authority outside of Scripture for an authoritative decision.

Other Protestants have said that the Holy Spirit will confirm the canon to Christians. If that is true, it would seem that all Christians should be able to identify the canon and thus agree on it. But all Christians do not agree on it—not even the Reformers among themselves!

And yet we can agree that the Holy Spirit *has* led God's people to recognize the canon—through the Church, under his guidance. The Church came into existence forty to sixty years before the New Testament was even complete. The writers of the New Testament already exercised their authority in the Church and were writing the New Testament even as they handed on that authority to others (e.g., see the books of 1 and 2 Timothy and Titus). Because the leaders of the Church had received the Sacred Tradition of the apostolic faith, they could determine the canon of Scripture without it needing to be said that they ruled over it.

A Protestant may try to escape the force of this principle by saying that the Church did not determine but merely discovered the biblical canon.[7] This would miss the point, however. Catholics do not argue that the Church made the individual books of Scripture become the word of God![8] Rather, they simply point out the fact that the Church made the authoritative list of inspired books, and regardless of how it can allegedly be reverse engineered, no individual has the authority to change it.[9] Now, this canon is either fallible or infallible. If the Church was fallible when it made this list, then it seems the canon itself is fallible. If not, then we have at least one instance of infallibility outside of Sacred Scripture.

A failure to take seriously the history of the biblical canon along with skepticism of the authority of the Church have tested the faith of many evangelicals—even scholars. As Protestant writer James Sawyer observed, "The conservative American evangelical apologetic for the shape of the New Testament canon has been historically the weakest link in its bibliology."[10] If the Church cannot be trusted, then the Bible is nothing but "a fallible collection of infallible books" (as R.C. Sproul famously observed). How can we place our faith in that?

But if we believe in faith that God meant for us to have an inspired Scripture that we could fully trust—both in its contents and its "table of contents"—then it should not be a great leap for us to all agree that the Holy Spirit could give infallible authority to the early Church to determine the true canon against a huge variety of possible false ones.

IN PRINCIPLE

PROTESTANTS AGREE: God willed to guide the determination of the canon so that Christians could have an accurate, inspired Bible.

IN PARTICULAR

CATHOLICISM AFFIRMS: God infallibly guided the Church in its determination of the canon.

Creeds and Councils

The difficulty of identification is not the only problem faced by those who wish to make the Bible alone their religious authority—the foundational Reformation principle of *sola scriptura*. For even if the authority of the biblical canon could somehow be affirmed without affirming the authority of the Church that determined it, there remains the matter of understanding what the Bible *means*. As we will see, much of what counts as an orthodox interpretation of the Bible is also grounded in the authority of the Church.

In theology, *orthodoxy* (from the Greek for "right teaching") refers to an authoritative standard. Historically speaking, orthodoxy has been determined by authoritative Church councils and communicated through its creeds. For example, even before the canon of Scripture was settled with any finality, the Church affirmed Jesus' divinity at the Council of Nicaea (A.D. 325) and eventually codified it in the Nicene Creed that up to today remains a faith standard for most Christians.

For Protestants, however, *sola scriptura* requires even the Church's councils and creeds to be subordinate to Scripture. The Bible by itself is the ultimate standard for orthodoxy, not decisions made by Church leaders. A problem with making the Bible the standard for orthodoxy, though, is that it is often *orthodoxy itself* that helps us understand what the Bible is saying. (For example, most Christians believe in the divinity of Christ, so for them, any interpretation of the Bible that denies his divinity can't be orthodox.) Thus, *sola scriptura* is itself dependent on a correct interpretive procedure—which of course the Bible itself doesn't provide, and which over the centuries has increasingly become a matter of debate among Christians.

Since the Bible does not tell us how to interpret it (and for that matter, neither does it say that it is the sole rule of faith), any Protestant's attempt to rely on the Bible alone *necessarily* relies on influences outside the Bible. In the end, Protestants are just as dependent on extrabiblical authority (the teaching of their pastor, Bible study leader, denomination founder, etc., or their own personal judgment) as are Catholics.

This helps to explain the hundreds of theological and interpretive disagreements among well-meaning Protestants over matters great and small. Although most Protestants are trying their best to make the Bible alone their religious authority, because the Bible is really a collection of books that must be interpreted, *their interpretation of the Bible* ends up being the real authority. For a host of subjective reasons, what seems clear to one will not be to another.[11]

Because the Catholic has a living Church that can communicate in more or less real time, the interpretive difficulty poses far fewer problems.[12] Although there is religious disagreement within Catholicism, it's rarely because the Church has not been clear in its teaching—rather, it is because the teaching allows for some difference of opinion or because people simply disagree with what it teaches.

Of course, none of this by itself makes the Church correct. Even if Catholicism presents a more ideal system than that of Protestantism, if the Church's Magisterium (the authoritative interpretive body of the Church) is no more trustworthy than anyone else, then all it does is push the problem back a step. For now, it is enough to note that both Catholics and Protestants go outside the pages of Scripture alone in order to arrive at an authoritative interpretation of it.

It is interesting to note that, as with the canon of Scripture, most Protestants continue to (indirectly) recognize the authority of the Catholic Church when, in most matters of orthodoxy, they affirm the rulings of the Church's councils and the statements of its creeds to inform their biblical interpretation. Doctrines that took hundreds of years to work out in detail are not simply being ascertained from the biblical text by Protestant interpreters with a couple years of seminary under their belt! As we have noted, there is an unspoken nod to a body of orthodox beliefs that were considered, debated, and declared (against many possible alternatives) in the early centuries of the Church.

In order to function as a religious authority, the Bible must be interpreted. But the Bible is often not easy to interpret. Protestants and Catholics agree that God wants us to draw only truth from the Bible and never falsehood. Jesus promised that the Church he built would not fail (Matt. 16:18)—yet it would if it fell into religious error (cf. Matt. 28:18–20). We also agree, at least in practice, that we all apply some standard or tradition when we interpret Scripture. Catholics simply go the extra step in recognizing God's protecting hand over his teaching Church, safeguarding the Bible from wrong interpretations and Christians from doctrinal error.

IN PRINCIPLE

PROTESTANTS AGREE: God wills to guide Christians into orthodoxy, including in the interpretation of Scripture, in ways that can include the teaching of pastors, scholars, and authors.

IN PARTICULAR

CATHOLICISM AFFIRMS: God does guide Christians into orthodoxy, and does so infallibly, by guiding the Church as it teaches and interprets Scripture.

The Unfailing Pope?

It's time to talk about the pope—or, rather, the office of the papacy. The papacy is not an extra layer in the Church's hierarchy, something to which you're ordained like a deacon, priest, or bishop. Rather, it's an office with special *charisms* or gifts. The pope is the bishop of Rome, and that comes with some status and privileges that other bishops do not enjoy. It also comes with a special gift from God known as *infallibility*.

The doctrine of papal infallibility says that when the pope is speaking on matters of faith or morals and is doing so in an authoritative way as the head of the Church, what he decrees is free from theological error. Although this sounds like a grand statement, it is actually a rather narrow claim.

For example, it does not mean that the pope's private opinions are safeguarded from mistakes. It also does not mean that a pope cannot sin. It doesn't mean that a pope will always teach what is needed at a given time and in the best possible way. The vast majority of papal actions, in fact, do not fall under the protection of infallibility. Popes can go and have gone their entire pontificates without invoking this charism.

A pope could hold personally to some pretty extreme views—even false ones—in many areas outside of faith or morals. A pope could even be personally wrong about something in the theological or moral realm so long as he never publicly decreed it to be part of the Faith. And a pope could be a seriously immoral individual without threatening the doctrine of infallibility. Although all these qualifications might seem to some Protestants as ways to weasel out of a problematic doctrine, or make infallibility practically pointless, they actually show that the Catholic Church is really not asking any more for papal infallibility than Protestants ask for the biblical writers.

The apostle Peter is a good example. Here is a man who, throughout the course of only a couple years with Jesus, managed to amass an impressive collection of embarrassing ministerial mistakes. These missteps climaxed when, in a single night, he sliced off someone's ear and denied Jesus three times. Yet the same man converted 3,000 people during his first sermon and later wrote two inspired, inerrant biblical letters.

Now, if a skeptic were to come along to a Protestant and say that the epistles of first and second Peter could not be trusted because of the ministerial and moral mistakes that the apostle Peter made during his life, most Protestants would have no difficulty answering with the distinction between the charism that God grants to the scriptural writers when they are in the course of writing and how they might live their lives otherwise. It is the same with papal infallibility. Because it is limited to only certain categories of situations, anything a pope says or does outside those categories cannot be used to argue against it.

Of course, it is one thing to defend the charism of infallibility for one of the apostles; it is quite another to do the same for all popes over the centuries. Indeed, the Catholic Church does not teach that the successors of the apostles (those men that the apostles chose to succeed them in their ministries), or even Peter's successors (the popes) have the same graces that the apostles did. When the pope speaks infallibly, he doesn't do so under direct inspiration from God as the biblical authors did when they wrote.

But then, Protestants also grant a charism of infallibility to the *non-apostles* who wrote the New Testament. Mark, for example, was not an apostle; neither was Luke. If God can give not only apostles but associates in their ministry a grace of infallible teaching in their writing, he certainly can do the same for associates in apostolic ministry (by succession) in their teaching.

The question, of course, is whether God actually did that. Catholics believe it is part of Jesus' promise that the Church wouldn't fail (Matt. 16:18) and that Jesus would protect Peter in a special way so that he could strengthen the rest of the Church (Luke 22:31–32). For Protestants, we could begin by pointing out that without some special grace of error-free judgment being given to the Church in some way, we could never know for sure that we have a correct and complete biblical canon. If God could protect the biblical authors from error in what they wrote and the early Church from assembling an erroneous Bible, why could he not protect a successor of the apostles from teaching religious error?

Besides, many Protestants today believe the Holy Spirit guides them personally. Evangelicals and Pentecostals, for example, often refer to the Spirit's guidance or God speaking to them so regularly that it becomes unremarkable. They believe God's grace can come into their hearts and lead them to right decisions or to the right interpretation or use of a Scripture passage.

Catholics can agree with Protestants that the Holy Spirit is active in the Church: guiding, consoling, advocating. The papacy and its protection of infallibility is just a special, formal example of that.

IN PRINCIPLE

PROTESTANTS AGREE: The Holy Spirit moved fallible sinners to infallibly produce Scripture and choose a biblical canon, and even today moves people to make correct decisions and interpretations.

CATHOLICISM AFFIRMS: The Holy Spirit protects the fallible, sinful successors of St. Peter from teaching religious or moral errors.

Checking Your Brains at the Door?

Some Protestants worry that having an infallible authority in the Church means that Christians are not supposed to think for themselves. But skeptics and atheists say the exact same thing about the Bible. Any time an authority is involved in a belief system, the same complaint can be made.

I remember a professor at Westminster Theological Seminary introducing the topic of Catholic authority to his Protestant students by telling them that he once asked a nun what she believed concerning some doctrinal question within the Church. The nun answered that she was waiting for the Church to tell her what she believed! The students in the class had a good laugh, but I wondered if any of them ever realized that they are actually in a very similar boat. Just as Catholics trust God's word revealed through the Church to tell them what to believe, Protestants trust God's word revealed in the Bible (the Church's book!) to tell them what to believe.

Unless someone simply makes up his own religion out of nothing, *every believer* believes what he believes on someone or something else's authority. That's what faith is.[13] Catholics may say that they let the Church tell them what to believe, Protestants might say they let the Bible tell them what to believe, and in principle these two only differ by the *object* of religious authority, not religious authority itself. Furthermore, as we have seen, in trusting the Bible as their religious authority, Protestants are actually trusting the Church as well.

PROTESTANTS AGREE: Having an infallible religious authority (the Bible) does not mean Christians can stop thinking.

CATHOLICISM AFFIRMS: Having an infallible religious authority (the Church) does not mean Christians can stop thinking.

Although there are many individual disagreements between Catholics and Protestants, the number-one issue is really the source of religious authority. We have seen that many of the specific issues that Protestants take with Catholic authority would, in principle, also undermine their own—and that many basic ideas about authority that Protestants share are fully compatible with Catholicism.

Agreeing only in principle, however, will not suffice for Christian unity. Agreement on which authority to submit to is a necessary condition for worshiping with one accord. As we will see in the next chapter, although the Christian's specific authority is often considered an insuperably divisive issue between Catholics and Protestants, we may be closer to common assent than we seem.

2

Scripture and Tradition

Catholicism teaches that the doctrines contained in Sacred Scripture (the Bible) and Sacred Tradition (the Church) are authoritative because God's revelation is the source of both. The *Catechism* puts it this way: "Sacred Tradition and Sacred Scripture make up a single sacred deposit of the word of God" (97). This means that "both Scripture and Tradition must be accepted and honored with equal sentiments of devotion and reverence" (82).

To some Protestants, this might sound blasphemous. The idea that *anything* the Church says could be on the same level as Scripture just doesn't make sense. After all, only the Bible was inspired by God, right? How, then, can Catholics say that both must be reverenced equally?

More importantly, what happens if they come into conflict? The Protestant, in principle, does not face these difficulties because the Bible is said to hold the supreme place. As the ultimate and final level of religious authority, according to *sola scriptura,* when the Bible comes into conflict with any other authority it must be declared the winner.

"Where Is That in the Bible?"

Protestants hold to subtly different forms of *sola scriptura*. At one end of the spectrum, it is thought to mean that only the Bible may be trusted as a source for faith and practice—and so everything the Christian believes must be explicitly found in it. On the other end, it means that the Bible is simply the *most trustworthy* source, and so no teachings can explicitly contradict it.

Protestants' objections to Catholic claims about Sacred Tradition will vary depending on which version of *sola scriptura* they hold. Some will argue that any addition of Tradition to the Bible is illicit, others will only see a problem if a particular tradition goes against Scripture. Either way though, Protestants are generally uncomfortable with an authoritative, big-T Church Tradition because they think it threatens the authority of Scripture.[14]

Some Catholics assume that by *sola scriptura* Protestants mean anything not found in the Bible is off-limits for Christian faith and practice. This is not what it originally meant, but it is the way the principle is often understood by those on the more Fundamentalist end of the spectrum.[15] Most Protestants, though, realize that to hold such a position would be self-defeating. This is because if one believes that everything a Christian is to believe or practice must be taught in the Bible, then the teaching that everything a Christian is to believe or practice must be taught in the Bible—but it isn't.

Although some apologists for this more extreme version of *sola scriptura* may point to verses such as 2 Timothy 3:16–17—which says that all Scripture is inspired and useful—for support, such appeals to prooftexts are unconvincing. Nowhere in the Bible does it say clearly that *Scripture alone is the source for all Christian faith and practice*. Thus, Protestants who hold to any form of *sola scriptura* thereby show that at least *one* Christian belief (or two, if you include the canon) can be derived from something besides the Bible itself.

IN PRINCIPLE

PROTESTANTS AGREE: Not everything that Christians are to believe must be taught explicitly in Scripture.

IN PARTICULAR

CATHOLICISM AFFIRMS: Some things that Christians are to believe have been taught outside of Scripture.

Most Protestants do, in fact, believe in the authority of some kind of tradition. Virtually every Protestant denomination has some sort of confession or doctrinal statement that members must adhere to in order to be identified as members. But these denominations cannot authoritatively compel faith in these confessions, and if a given Protestant disagrees and can back that up with his interpretation of Scripture, it's his duty to follow that interpretation even if it means leaving the church.

This, essentially, is the history of Protestantism. In the sixteenth century, when Martin Luther determined that the Catholic Church had gotten its teaching on salvation wrong and that his belief in *sola fide* or salvation by faith alone was the correct, biblical view,[16] he refused to submit this private interpretation to the Church's authority. This is summarized in his famous statement at the Diet of Worms:

Unless I am convinced by the testimony of the scriptures or by clear reason (for I do not trust either in the pope or in councils alone, since it is well-known that they have often erred and contradicted themselves), I am bound by the scriptures I have quoted and my conscience is captive to the word of God. . . . I cannot do otherwise, here I stand, may God help me, amen.[17]

The problem with this principle, Luther soon learned, is that the "testimony of the scriptures" can be read in numerous ways. Once he opened the door for every individual's reasoning to become his religious authority, it was impossible to close it again without destroying the foundation of his own movement. Private interpretation turned out to be every bit as fallible as Protestants thought the Church's was, and within decades Protestantism had splintered into disagreeing factions all centered on their individual interpretations of Scripture.

Thus Protestantism replaced the authority of the Church with the authority of the individual. With no infallible authority to judge it, a denomination's level of authority was only as strong as the level of agreement it had with its members.

When I was a Protestant, we joked that Protestantism "multiplied by dividing." By enshrining private interpretation as the final arbiter of Christian truth, *sola scriptura* is a recipe for endless fracture. But even within it we can find opportunities for accord with Catholics.

The Bible Is Never Alone

It must be recognized that most Protestants do not have a problem with the idea that God's revelation can take more than one form.

In his letter to the Romans, St. Paul writes, "What can be known about God is plain to them, because God has shown it to them. Ever since the creation of the world his invisible nature, namely, his eternal power and deity, has been clearly perceived in the things that have been made" (1:19–20). Paul seems to be echoing the Old Testament book of Wisdom, which says, "For from the greatness and beauty of created things comes a corresponding perception of their Creator" (13:5). All of this agrees with the psalmist, who declared that "the heavens are telling the glory of God; and the firmament proclaims his handiwork" (Ps. 19:1).

So we see in Scripture itself that God reveals himself (clearly and to all people) through his creation, *apart from Scripture*. Theologians call this kind of revelation *natural* (because it comes through nature) or *general* (because it is given to all people). In contrast, revelation that is given by prophetic utterances or recorded in inspired writings is called *supernatural* (because it is direct communication from God) or *special* (because it is not available to all people without qualification).

Catholics and Protestants agree that these two modes of revelation are both legitimate and authoritative—at least in theory. In its two millennia on earth, the Catholic Church has developed many careful distinctions, one of them being to subdivide supernatural, public revelations into those originally written (Sacred Scripture) and unwritten (Sacred Tradition). Catholics emphasize that all truth is "God's truth" and therefore that no revelation can truly contradict another, whereas Protestants elevate the written form above the others. But Protestants will agree that God can and does reveal himself in ways outside the pages of the Bible.

IN PRINCIPLE

PROTESTANTS AGREE: God's revelation comes to us in more than the written form.

CATHOLICISM AFFIRMS: God's public, special revelation has come to us in written and unwritten form.

An important thing to note here is that regardless of their source, written words need to be interpreted. Language is a set of signs (whether oral or written) pointing to things in reality. Therefore, our knowledge of reality will determine our interpretation of words. When I say or write the word *dog*, English speakers will know what I mean because we have agreed that this word refers to the animal we all recognize as a dog.

That's pretty straightforward, but language is not always that easy to understand. *Dog* can also refer to a person (usually, but not always, in a negative way) or it can be a word to modify a type of day in summer or express how tired I am.

Aside from the challenge of words having multiple definitions, sometimes the same meaning is applied to distinct things in very specific ways. For example, if I say, "My wife is a peach," no one would suspect that I had married a fruit! Instinctively, they would compare what they know about peaches and women to what I had said and infer my actual meaning ("My wife is sweet"). This is as true of the Bible as anything else.[18]

For example, the words of Scripture describe our planet as being circular (Isa. 40:22) and as having corners (Rev. 7:1). Because something cannot be both circular and cornered, it seems clear that one of these verses was meant to be taken metaphorically. But which one? One could argue from genre types or try to dig into the original Hebrew and Greek, but in our age it is much easier to consult natural revelation (simply look at the planet!).

Another example that hits closer to home is the nature of God himself. Christians believe that God is spirit and that he is not limited by a body. Now, we have a good proof-text for this view in John 4:24 (cf. Luke 24:39). However, if someone wanted to argue that God does have a body, he could find plenty of support in Scripture, which regularly speaks of God having a body with which to sit (Ps. 47:8), walk (Gen. 3:8), or give off odor (Num. 28:2), as well as bodily parts such as an arm (Isa. 52:10), hand (Exod. 33:22), eyes (Prov. 15:3), and even wings (Ps. 91:4).

In this case it's not a simple matter of discerning between the literal and metaphorical, because we do not have the kind of direct knowledge of God that we have of his creation. We haven't seen God, so perhaps he does have wings! Although philosophy helps us figure out some of God's attributes (for example, that he is pure spirit), this can require specialized knowledge and time for careful thought, so at first glance we have no reason not to entertain a literal interpretation of these verses.

But Catholics believe that God has provided authoritative Tradition through the Church to safeguard the faithful from misunderstanding; a body of truths, revealed by Christ and passed on by the apostles to the Church, that help us interpret the words of Scripture.

As we noted, Protestants are practically in the same boat but do not always speak as if they appreciate it. Some will grant that tradition is important and not to be ignored, but usually with the qualification that it must always be judged in light of Scripture. Of course, in order to judge tradition by Scripture, we must know what Scripture teaches—and that requires interpretation! What this mindset effectively leads to is either unbending confidence in one's interpretation (despite numerous disagreements), or an acceptance of any understanding that at least doesn't expressly contradict Scripture's broadest and most general points.

Along with recognition of the Church's teaching authority, belief in Sacred Tradition as an additional form of revelation allows Catholics to be much more comfortable with the ambiguity of Scripture. It is the nature of language that it can be understood in numerous ways, and when you add to the mix gaps in translation, culture, philosophy, geography, and other areas, it is unsurprising when multiple conflicting interpretations of an ancient text arise. This is why the Catholic Church does not affirm *sola scriptura*—not because the Bible is somehow deficient, but because its wording is not sufficient to limit itself to only one understanding.[19]

IN PRINCIPLE

PROTESTANTS AGREE: God's written revelation is often interpreted by his revelation through other sources, such as creation and the historical Christian tradition.

IN PARTICULAR

CATHOLICISM AFFIRMS: God's written revelation is interpreted by his revelation in creation and Tradition.

No better proof of this claim is needed than a survey of the beliefs of groups holding to *sola scriptura*. Although some Protestants chafe at exaggerated claims that Catholic apologists occasionally make about the number of Protestant groups and the depths of their division, it's manifest that within Protestantism there are many real disagreements across the spectrum of their doctrinal commitments and at every level of importance. Even the Reformation principle of *sola fide* is disputed because what counts as "justification," as "faith," and as "alone" are all understood in different ways by various theological camps.[20] Or witness the sharpening divisions between Protestant groups that affirm traditional biblical teachings about marriage and sex and those that reinterpret Scripture on these matters to fit the spirit of the age.

There are, of course, disputes within Catholicism as well—but many of these are examples of *dissent,* not of differing private interpretations lacking the possibility of authoritative settlement. A good example of this process is found in Acts chapter 15. Here we read that a doctrinal disagreement had arisen over non-Jewish participation in the life of the Church. The question was whether or not Gentiles (non-Jews) had to be initiated into the Mosaic covenant if they were to be considered true Christians. While we are able to predict the outcome now that it has been settled for centuries, it is important to realize that the solution to this problem was not evident at the time. Lacking any direct, special revelation on the subject, the apostles could not simply grab a Bible concordance and start quoting prooftexts! Instead, they gathered with others in a council and, drawing on the teachings of Jesus as well as their own experiences, firmly settled the matter. Although they did not have clear scriptural tradition to draw from (and indeed, Scripture seemed to indicate the opposite of their conclusion), the apostles concluded that the Holy Spirit had guided their decision (Acts 15:28). Once this intra-Church dispute was settled, it became part of Christian orthodoxy and was no longer legitimately disputable. The Catholic Church has not departed from this biblical process over its two millennia of existence.[21]

Biblical Non-Biblical Traditions

We don't even have to appeal to extrabiblical doctrines or events to find accord with Protestants on the validity of extrabiblical traditions—we can just use Scripture. In the New Testament, there are numerous affirmations of extra-biblical traditions:

- The Old Testament does not name the magicians in Egypt who tried to discredit Moses, but Paul calls them Jannes and Jambres (2 Tim. 3:8).

- Jude expects his readers to be aware that Michael the Archangel disputed with Satan over the body of Moses (verse 9) and that Enoch prophesied Christ (verses 14–15), but these stories are found nowhere else in Scripture.

- The writer of the book of Hebrews (11:37) talks about Old Testament saints being sawn in half for their faith—but he didn't get this from the Old Testament.

And it is not just New Testament references to the Old Testament that seem to go beyond the Bible. In Acts 20:35, Paul quotes Jesus as saying, "It is more blessed to give than to receive"—yet Jesus is not recorded as having said this anywhere in the Gospels. It seems apparent that the New Testament writers were not afraid to reference extrabiblical traditions.[22] This does not, of course, raise extrabiblical traditions to the level of inspiration—but it does show that unwritten traditions can be infallibly affirmed.

IN PRINCIPLE

PROTESTANTS AGREE: Traditions not recorded in Scripture can be infallibly affirmed (by Scripture).

IN PARTICULAR

CATHOLICISM AFFIRMS: Traditions not recorded in Scripture can be infallibly affirmed (by the Church).

Traditions of [Protestant] Men

It is not uncommon to hear Protestants complain that Catholics added unbiblical traditions to what the Bible teaches. Sometimes they will even cite scriptures that disparage man-made traditions (e.g., Matthew 15:3–6).[23] Doesn't holding to traditions not taught by the Bible nullify the word of God?

The first thing to note here is that there is a big difference between something being non-biblical and it being *anti-*biblical. Owning a cell phone is non-biblical; worshiping an idol is anti-biblical. Simply not appearing in the Bible doesn't make something false.

Moreover, numerous facets of Protestant worship are based on a denomination's tradition rather than anything affirmed or commanded in Scripture. For example, the idea of youth pastors, worship bands, meeting in church build-ings, or sitting in pews has no explicit support in Scripture.[24]

Most Protestants, however, recognize that not all Christian beliefs and practices are spelled out in the Bible. They realize that there is development and religious thought and that these sometimes lead to affirmations that, though extrabiblical, are nonetheless authoritative. To believe otherwise would be to reject the Church's explanation of the Trinity at the Council of Nicaea, or the Council of Chalcedon's definition of the incar-nation of Jesus Christ. Indeed, it would threaten Protestantism itself, which is a development that did not come to exist until the sixteenth century. The real problem, then, comes when a religious group teaches something that is contrary to the Bible.

IN PRINCIPLE

PROTESTANTS AGREE: We can affirm beliefs and practices that aren't explicitly in Scripture but developed over time.

IN PARTICULAR

CATHOLICISM AFFIRMS: The Church can teach doc-trine and prescribe practices that aren't explicitly found in Scripture but developed over time.

Sometimes differing biblical interpretations contradict each other, but other times they're just different without logically ruling each other out. By the same token, some-times a biblical interpretation is different from the literal words of a Bible verse but does not logically contradict it.

Protestants acknowledge this. A good example is James 2:24. In most translations the verse reads, "A man is justified by works and not by faith alone." (This verse is the only place in Scripture where the words *justified, works, faith,* and *alone* appear together.)[25] Despite these seemingly clear words, Martin Luther launched the Protestant Reformation with a doctrine that contradicts them—namely, *sola fide,* belief that justification is by faith alone apart from works.

Most Protestants are not unaware of this problem, and they have come up with various ways of explaining James 2:24 that fit with their theology. The important thing here is not who is right or who is wrong—but simply that if Protestants claim they can legitimately theologize their way out of directly contradicting the words of Scripture, then in theory Catholics can do it too. Otherwise they are engaging in what logicians call *special pleading*—applying different principles to similar cases in order to avoid appearing wrong.

Tardy Traditions

Even if it is admitted in principle that both Catholics and Protestants accept extrabiblical traditions and that both sides have interpretations that only *apparently* contradict Scripture, it still seems problematic to many Protestants that Catholics accept traditions with late dates in history. It is one thing to accept the fourth-century determination of the canon of Scripture or the creeds that delineate orthodoxy; it is quite another for Catholics to affirm doctrines that were not defined until relatively recent times.

As with many other allegedly principled disagreements between Catholics and Protestants, there is an inconsistency here—but it is more subtle than others and based on one's understanding of "tradition." When the Church speaks of tradition, it does not only mean time-honored teachings or practices. As we noted, it refers to non-written religious authority (whatever its source). So, a teaching held by the Church since the fourth century is tradition, but so is one defined in the twentieth. Both the Nicene Council of A.D. 325 and the Vatican II Council of 1965 possess ecclesial and historical traditional authority—the Nicene Council just has a longer history behind it.

Moreover, Catholic dogma is always related very closely to the original "deposit of faith"—the teachings (written in Scripture and taught orally in Sacred Tradition) revealed by Christ and taught by the apostles. Here is where the idea of historical development becomes critical. The trinitarian definitions of Nicaea were a development (not a distortion!) of the Church's historic teachings about the nature of Jesus Christ. Although the Church did not technically teach "the Trinity" in the first or second centuries, the dogma was not "new" teaching in the fourth—it was simply an elucidation of what the Church believed based on other things it taught clearly.

Catholics do not believe that this sort of authoritative doctrinal development ceased with the death of the apostles or even in the first millennium. Rather, one of the purposes of the Church demands that this practice continue. Jesus did far more than was recorded in Scripture (John 21:25) and many truths were left to be worked out in the future after he ascended to heaven (e.g., Acts 15; 1 Cor. 7:12). Those who deny this principle must say where to draw the line, and justify it. If it is legitimate for a group to deny what the Church taught about the Eucharist at the Council of Trent, then why is it not legitimate to deny what the Church defined as canonical Scripture or taught about the hypostatic union or the Trinity at Chalcedon or Nicaea?

IN PRINCIPLE

PROTESTANTS AGREE: We can profess doctrines that took centuries to develop and be defined.

IN PARTICULAR

CATHOLICISM AFFIRMS: Some doctrines took *many* centuries to be defined in detail, but they are nonetheless authoritative and part of historical Christian belief.

The doctrine of papal infallibility suffers from the complaint of historical latency, not being defined until the nineteenth century. It is, however, founded on other settled doctrines and historical facts that can be traced back to the early Church. This is how doctrinal development works.

When the Church declared that the bishop of Rome taught infallibly under certain conditions, it was not simply codifying longstanding affirmations of the pope's teaching authority. It was safeguarding theologically significant events of the past that might be cast into doubt without a "buck-stopping" authority to validate them. For example, if we could never be certain of which Church rulings were in agreement with the Holy Spirit (cf. Acts 15:28), we could never be sure of the canon of Scripture, or of the dogma of the Trinity, or doctrines concerning the Incarnation. The declaration of the infallibility of the pope was therefore an explanation of historical realities—not a doctrine cut from whole cloth.

And this is not unusual in the history of the Church. The Jerusalem Council's decision in Acts 15 was not based on biblical arguments, but by the need to explain the common experience of the apostles. At the Council of Nicaea, it was not just Scripture but also the traditional worship of the Church that was brought together to support and form the doctrine of the Trinity. This is also how doctrinal development works.

The dogmatic assertion of papal infallibility was followed quickly by two more definitions that were declared in order to deepen our understanding of beliefs that had already become part of the Church's faith and practice. The immaculate conception of Mary and her assumption into heaven are the only dogmas defined infallibly by a pope since his infallibility became dogma.

Now, these two dogmas may not seem to be taught in Scripture or by the very early Church (although Mary's *dormition*, later called the *Assumption* in the West, has roots in the sixth century and was well accepted 700 years before it became defined dogma). On the surface they seem to be in quite a different category from the venerable doctrines of the Trinity or the Incarnation, making these nineteenth-century definitions examples of doctrinal *distortion* rather than development. Although a detailed examination of the history of these dogmas is beyond our scope here, it's important to note that neither of these beliefs simply sprang on the scene fully formed in the last couple hundred years. They are the full flower of seeds that were planted and sprouted much further back in history.

That some of these dogmas were subjects of dispute shouldn't concern the Christian faithful. Most dogmas, in fact, were finally defined precisely because they *were* disputed! We see this beginning in Scripture in Acts 15—the so-called Council of Jerusalem to which we alluded earlier. Although the idea that a non-Jewish Christian would need to follow Jewish ritual laws seems obviously false today, in the early Church it was a seriously debated question (and one that, notably, was *not* settled by appealing to Scripture alone).

The canon of Scripture itself came as a result of false teachings. One of the first Christian heretics, Marcion, became a fiercely anti-Semitic teacher. In support of his beliefs, Marcion declared that the true scriptures were limited to the Gospel of Luke and several New Testament epistles.[26] Now at this time, no official canon of Sacred Scripture existed—but that did not mean the Church was confused about whether or not the Old Testament, the Gospel of Matthew, or St. Paul's letters to Timothy belonged in the Bible! Later synods and councils, such as those at Rome, Hippo, and Carthage, addressed the issue of the canon—but again, these were reactive recordings of what the Church already recognized—not brand new decisions.

After the canon of Scripture was closed, the Church continued to hold such meetings. The Council of Nicaea was called to deal with a dispute over the nature of God's Son. Although no legitimate Christian group today denies that Jesus Christ is fully God, at the time of the council a large faction of Christians, including many leaders, were teaching that heresy.[27] The traditional belief in Christ's divinity had to be settled with clear language, and the Church acted—by meeting in council and producing authoritative judgments. It was not as though the Church's faith was up in the air until that point—this judgment was dealing with a new false teaching that went against what the Church taught.

A similar example is the detailed explication of Jesus' incarnation at the Council of Chalcedon. Although the Church had always taught that Jesus was both God and man, the details had not all been declared and that left the teaching open to various misunderstandings. When some of these mistakes began to take hold, the Church acted decisively to correct them. Once again, it was not as though the divinity or humanity of Jesus was in serious question or that a new dogma was being developed. Rather, the Church's authoritative declaration came as a reaction to new errors.

The same Church that held these councils and declared these dogmas continues to exist and hold similar councils today. The difficulty Protestants must face is how to consistently and principally accept the above councils while rejecting others (such as the second Council of Nicaea which declared that icons could be properly reverenced).

IN PRINCIPLE

PROTESTANTS AGREE: Councils were sometimes necessary to authoritatively settle theological debates.

IN PARTICULAR

CATHOLICISM AFFIRMS: Councils continue to be necessary to authoritatively settle theological debates.

Questionable Translations

When people speak of "Catholic" or "Protestant" Bibles, they are usually referring to the list of books included in each. Some, however, are asking about specific translations. While there really is no official "Catholic" translation, some are preferred over others.

Some may question the propriety of declaring one translation over another—especially because it would be easy to fool non-linguists with faulty translations that favor the teachings of one group over another.[28] This accusation is often leveled against translations that call Mary "full of grace" at Luke 1:28. This sounds a bit too "Catholic" especially since it is the common English translation of the rosary prayer. First, this translation comes from the Revised Standard Version—a Catholic favorite, to be sure—but one that was the result of a committee of the National Council of the Churches of Christ in the United States of America. Further, the more popular Catholic translation (the New American Bible) has "Hail, favored one!" here.

There is, however, a more troublesome example from the Protestant world. Romans 3:28 is the closest verse in Scripture that Martin Luther could find to support his novel idea concerning justification by faith alone.[29] However, it lacked that all important word "alone" that would support his "sola" doctrine. So, Luther added the word "alone" to his German translation of Romans 3:28 ("man is justified by faith alone apart from the deeds of the law")! It seems, then, that Luther himself was guilty of doing the very thing he accused the Catholic Church of doing: elevating his theology above the Bible (violating *sola scriptura* in order to support *sola fide*).

Bias in biblical translation is an undesirable fact of life for both Catholics and Protestants. Both sides can come up with "gotcha" examples where theological bias seems to have overruled good translation practices, but these are rather rare and should not be considered evidence of conspiracy for either group.[30] As both sides can agree, there is no perfect Bible translation and several should be consulted when doing serious Bible study.

IN PRINCIPLE

PROTESTANTS AGREE: Biased biblical translations are not welcome, but they do not necessarily make the teachings false.

IN PARTICULAR

CATHOLICISM AFFIRMS: Biased biblical translations are not welcome, but they do not necessarily make Catholic teachings false.

Apocryphal Additions

When teaching *Introduction to the New Testament* at my Evangelical seminary, I always got a kick out of starting the first class by asking the students to turn to 1 Maccabees. Reactions ranged from confusion to uncertain laughter—"Silly professor, that's a Catholic book!"

There are seven books and a few chapters of the Old Testament that were removed from the Protestant canon in modern Bibles. These include Wisdom, Sirach, Tobit, Judith, Baruch, 1–2 Maccabees, and chapters in Esther and Daniel). These are collectively known as the *deuterocanonical* books. The word *deuterocanon* simply means "second canon" and these books come after the Hebrew writings. Protestants, however, refer to this collection as the *Apocrypha,* which means "hidden."

Calling these books hidden is frankly unjustifiable, given that these writings are found in the Septuagint (the Greek translation of the Old Testament that the New Testament writers cited more often than the Hebrew) and *Codex Siniaticus* (the earliest Bible we have), as well as early Greek manuscripts such as Aleph, A, and B. Further, the Dead Sea Scrolls at Qumran (and Masada as well) include nearly seventy fragments from Tobit, several chapters from Sirach, and a small piece of the Epistle of Jeremiah (included in Baruch in the Catholic canon).

One argument, though, against regarding the deuterocanonicals as Scripture is the Protestant claim to follow the "Jewish canon," which excludes them. There are a few problems with this claim. First, the idea of a single Jewish canon is something of an anachronism. We see from the New Testament itself that at the time of Christ there were competing canons: the Sadducees accepted only the Torah (the first five books of the Old Testament) whereas the Pharisees followed the modern Jewish canon, and Jews outside Israel often followed the Septuagint. (And of course, the Jewish people left another twenty-seven books out of the biblical canon—namely the entire New Testament!)

Another popular argument against including the deuterocanonicals is that they are never quoted or mentioned in the New Testament. Although this might sound concerning, there are serious problems with this criterion. First, deuterocanonical material *is* referenced in the New Testament. In fact, the 1611 King James Version Bible (the most popular Protestant Bible of all time) contains over a hundred references to them in the Old Testament and eleven in the

New Testament. Even more impressive is the massive list supported by the Nestle-Aland Greek New Testament.

And if Old Testament *allusions* are acceptable even where a full quote is missing, the influence of the deuterocanonicals elsewhere in Scripture grows (e.g., clear allusions to Wisdom 5, 12, and 15 can be found in St. Paul's letter to the Romans).

Second, there are several other books in the Protestant canon (Ezra, Nehemiah, Esther, Ecclesiastes, the Song of Solomon, Judges, Ruth, Obadiah, Nahum, and Zephaniah) that aren't quoted elsewhere in Scripture, but Protestants retain them in their canon anyway. Finally, non-canonical and even pagan material *is* referenced in the New Testament. Besides the well-known use of the book of Enoch in Jude or the many pagan poets that Paul quotes, there are hundreds of other non-biblical references in the Bible.

These points of agreement over the criteria for canonicity, once brought to light, can be occasions for reaching greater accord on the matter of the canon of Scripture.

IN PRINCIPLE

PROTESTANTS AGREE: Old Testament books do not need to be quoted elsewhere in Scripture in order to be considered canon, and being alluded to or quoted in Scripture does not make a writing necessarily canonical.

IN PARTICULAR

CATHOLICISM AFFIRMS: That some deuterocanonical books are not quoted elsewhere in Scripture does not rule them out of the canon.

Yet another claim made by some Protestants against the deuterocanonicals is that none claim to be written by prophets.[31] But this argument is also counter-productive to the Protestant cause because, first, few of the New Testament authors are ever said to be prophets, and some were not even apostles (e.g., Mark, Luke). Furthermore, not all of the New Testament authors are even named in the original text—some are no longer even identifiable (such as the author of Hebrews). Even Protestants would, therefore, have to trust Church tradition to even get this "prophetic" criterion off the ground.

Finally, these criteria could exclude other Old Testament books as well—for example, 1–2 Chronicles and 1–2 Kings are not said to be written by prophets, and many books contain no predictive prophecy. Indeed, the Protestant version of Esther does not even mention God! If these facts do not exclude Old Testament books that Protestants accept, they should not be used to exclude the deuterocanonicals.[32]

IN PRINCIPLE

PROTESTANTS AGREE: Old Testament books do not need to be written by acknowledged prophets to be considered canonical.

IN PARTICULAR

CATHOLICISM AFFIRMS: The deuterocanonical books do not need to be written by acknowledged prophets to be considered canonical.

Other Protestants claim that the deuterocanonicals should be kept out of the biblical canon because they contain historical errors. Critical scholars use the same kind of argument against Old Testament books like Exodus and Daniel, and biblical apologists often blame copyist errors or faulty historians for such problems. Others point out that many passages in the Bible are parabolic or apocalyptic in nature and so are not to be taken in the literal sense that generates the problem.

For example, 2 Kings 8:26 says that Ahaziah was twenty-two years old when he became king, whereas 2 Chronicles 22:2 indicates that he was forty-two years old. In Mark's Gospel (2:26) it says that David "went into the house of God when Abiathar was high priest," but 1 Samuel 21:1 says that Ahimelech (Abiathar's father) was the high priest. Yet Protestants do not reject these books for these inconsistencies. So if it's legitimate to overlook small factual glitches for books in the Protestant canon, why can't this be done for the deuterocanonicals?

IN PRINCIPLE

PROTESTANTS AGREE: Biblical books that appear to make historical errors do not need to be removed from the canon, because these alleged errors can be explained.

IN PARTICULAR

CATHOLICISM AFFIRMS: Deuterocanonical books that appear to make historical errors do not need to be removed from the canon, because these alleged errors can be explained.

Other Protestant apologists claim that the deuterocanonicals can't be inspired because they make theological mistakes. Of course, identifying theological error can be a very subjective process. Catholics find support for purgatory and prayers for the dead in the deuterocanonical book 2 Maccabees (namely 12:39–45 and 15:12–16). But because Protestants consider these teachings unbiblical, for them that's a reason to exclude the book.

As you can probably see, this is a circular argument. It says that a deuterocanonical book isn't inspired because it contains a teaching that's not in the Bible . . . because it isn't inspired.

The founder of the Reformation, Martin Luther, considered the deuterocanonicals to be "good for reading" but not part of inspired Scripture (he did not actually remove them from his German Bible, though; he simply moved them to the end of the Old Testament). Though Protestants may applaud this conclusion, it should be remembered that Luther also argued for the removal of Esther because the Protestant version of it never mentions God, and he disliked the books of Hebrews, James, Jude, and Revelation for theological reasons as well. He deemed it impossible to harmonize James (who, as we saw, contradicted *sola fide*) and Paul, and characterized the letter of James as an "epistle of straw" that had "no evangelical character."[33]

It's hard for the Bible to be considered the sole theological authority for Christians if we let our theology determine what counts as the Bible. But since Protestants already acknowledge some books that are problematic for their theology, we are already on our way to reaching accord on the deuterocanonical books.

IN PRINCIPLE

PROTESTANTS AGREE: Books should not be omitted from the canon simply because they contain teachings that are difficult or that some Christians find objectionable.

There are more detailed arguments for the inclusion of each deuterocanonical book in the Bible. But even after considering these, it remains a fact that ultimately the Church had to make the call. For both Catholics and Protestants, a book's canonical status is ultimately grounded in Church tradition, and carefully examining Protestants' criteria for canonicity can actually help move them closer to seeing that.

Although Luther once confidently issued the challenge, "Come forward...and produce any one mystery which is still abstruse in the scriptures" and proudly proclaimed that "if many things still remain abstruse to many, this does not arise from obscurity in the scriptures, but from their own blindness or want of understanding," the fact is that Protestants today are divided in ways great and small on nearly as many issues as can be imagined.

What is the Protestant position on predestination? It depends on whether you ask a Calvinist or an Arminian. What is the Protestant position on women in ministry? It depends on if you ask an Egalitarian or a Complementarian. What is the Protestant position on justification by faith alone? It depends on whether you ask someone in the Lordship Salvation movement or the *Free Grace* movement. What is the Protestant position on moral issues such as abortion, homosexuality, or divorce? The answer again depends on which kind of Protestant you ask.

As we have seen, however, Protestants affirm numerous particular teachings that are based on the same foundational principles. They affirm that there is more than one way that God revealed himself to people and they believe in important traditions that are found outside of Scripture. Like certain Catholic doctrinal definitions, Protestantism itself is late to Church history, as are its twin foundational doctrines (one of which, *sola scriptura*, is not stated in Scripture and the other, *sola fide*, is in direct verbal contradiction with the only scriptural passage that uses its wording).

Catholics can come up with scriptural prooftexts for the Church's teachings just as Protestants do for their interpretations.[34] Contrary to most Protestant teaching, the Bible says:

- justification is by works and not by faith alone (James 2:24);

- baptism saves (1 Pet. 3:21);

- some sins are mortal and some are not (1 John 5:16–17);

- salvation can be lost (John 15:6; Rom. 11:22; Heb. 10:28–29);

- the Eucharist is literally Jesus' body and blood (John 6:54–55; 1 Cor. 11:27–29);

- forgiveness of sins comes through confession to God's representatives (Matt. 18:15–18; John 20:23);

- divorce and remarriage is unacceptable (Mark 10:11–12); and

- Peter is given the keys of heaven (Matt. 16:18–19).

Protestants can't respond, "That's not in the Bible" if they are to maintain credibility. Instead, their only recourse is to appeal to interpretation—their own personal interpretation, or their pastor's, or their denominational tradition's. But the best evidence that biblical interpretation cannot settle many theological matters is Protestantism itself. Under the banner of *sola scriptura*, Protestantism has failed to achieve doctrinal or practical unity. Instead of worshiping together in one accord, hundreds of disagreeing denominations and subgroups have been created in reaction to what are considered the false teachings or problematic practices of the others. Indeed, Protestants can often find more in common with Catholics than other Protestants!

The encouraging news is that if Protestants can find ways to tolerate this situation, those same ways can be applied to tolerating Catholic positions—and just maybe moving closer to full accord with the Church.

3

Worship and Sacraments

Along with many Protestants, I used to proudly proclaim that Christianity is not a *religion* but rather a *relationship*. I looked down on the poor souls attending churches that practiced rote religious ceremonies instead of promoting a vibrant living faith. I believed that God wanted to be my *friend* (John 15:15), not just my Lord (Matt. 7:21).

The idea is that "religion" is about man trying to earn heaven or get to God through his own efforts, whereas Christianity is about God reaching down to enter into relationship with mankind. In their eyes, Catholicism's worship practices amount to religious legalism—the substitution of rules for relationship. Catholics, it is thought, trade relationship for ritual.[35]

The Protestant attitude seems to be grounded in the idea that, by the time of Christ, Jewish worship had fallen into illicit legalism. Although this notion has come under fire recently even in Protestant circles,[36] it persists in the minds of many, leading them to the conclusion that ritual and good works are not only unhelpful but actually harmful to salvation, because they replace true, relational worship with false religious gestures.

In this account, it is not difficult to see Catholicism as a dead faith doomed to failure. *Those statues and necklaces aren't going to help you when you face God on Judgment Day!* I know that for me, Catholics seemed little more than fancy cult members. Sure, there were a lot of legalistic Protestants out there, but at least their legalism was confined to their church—it was not institutionalized and demanded like it was for Catholics.

When I got to know some faithful Catholics, though, my perspective changed. I saw genuine piety as well as a surprising focus on having a relationship with God. How that relationship looked and was maintained was often different, but in many cases the goal seemed to be the same. These folks were not trying to "earn heaven" through their devotions any more than a typical Protestant was by tithing or dressing in his Sunday best. In Catholicism I found that both religion and relationship were not seen as opposed to each other (James 1:27) but as things to be pursued together. I discovered I could be a faithful worker *for* God (2 Tim. 2:15) and a faithful friend *of* God at the same time. In fact, each is necessary for the other (James 2:21–24).

As we will see, the balance between ritual and relationship is not unique to Catholicism.

Worship Style and Structure

Although there are some Protestant denominations today that haven't done away with high liturgical practices, many of the more popular Evangelical groups, Baptists, Pentecostals, and nondenominational mixtures of these groups tend to see intricate liturgy as confining, and they pride themselves on the simplicity of their worship. Even so, as anyone who has been to a number of these worship services can tell you, they nearly always follow a discernible pattern. You might say, then, that even though they stripped down liturgy, they have a liturgy nonetheless.

For most of my Evangelical life, I attended either Calvary Chapel churches in California or Baptist churches in North Carolina. Although neither church would be (or want to be) considered liturgical, I knew what to expect every week. With surprisingly little variation between the two distinct kinds of churches, there was typically several regular stages: walking in, greeting, singing, seating, more singing, special performance, sermon, final song, announcements, and racing the other churches to lunch.

At the most stripped-down worship services, such as those practiced by Quakers who might sit in complete silence for up to an hour waiting for someone to speak, order and an expectation of process remain. Even in the most unstructured worship services, such as those in more extreme Pentecostal and charismatic churches, radical movements of God still tend to happen rather on cue. The fact is almost no churches are truly spontaneous in their worship. Whether it is justified merely practically (what human gathering can go very long without order?) or theologically (God is a God of order, after all—1 Cor. 14:33), or what it is called, even the most "spirit-led" churches follow discernible patterns.

IN PARTICULAR

CATHOLICISM AFFIRMS: Liturgy, especially the Mass, should follow a certain order that people can recognize and follow.

Images of God

One particular thing that seems to trouble many Protestants is the use of images in Catholic worship. Most Protestants are familiar with the commandment of God that says not to make a graven image (Exod. 20:4), and they see Catholic statuary—or paintings, or icons—as violations of it. This is part of the reason why the interior of most Protestant churches is typically devoid of such religious imagery (sometimes with the exception of stained-glass windows or felt banners). It is understandable, then, why many Protestants are uncomfortable with such things in Catholic churches.

Although it may seem obvious that putting a statue in a church is a violation of the "graven images" commandment, there is more to the story. First of all, the commandment says that "you shall not make for yourself a graven image, or any likeness of anything that is in heaven above, or that is in the earth beneath, or that is in the water under the earth" (Exod. 20:4). Note that the commandment does not limit the prohibition to religious images. It states that there can be no graven image made of *anything* in existence, yet Protestants typically do not have a problem with statues, sculptures, or images of non-religious objects outside a church. Indeed, most don't even have a problem with representations of crosses in a church, or of religious art (such as nativity sets)—especially when it is limited to public places or the home. The commandment, however, makes no such qualifications.

A second thing to note here is that the word *graven* implies something *carved*. Thus, it would not seem to apply to images that are drawn or painted (which is a good thing for Protestants who include such things in books and on t-shirts). This may be why many Protestant churches continue to install stained-glass windows or to hang photos, paintings, and banners in their places of worship.

When these two factors are put together, it does not seem that Protestants should have a problem with the presence of religiously representative objects. We'll get to their use in worship next, but for now it is enough to establish that—even for Protestants—the mere representation of religiously significant persons or things is not a violation of the commandment against making "graven images." Further, we can see that with some things at least, even their presence in churches is allowable.

IN PRINCIPLE

PROTESTANTS AGREE: The presence of religiously representative objects—even three-dimensional ones carved out of various materials—is allowable in public places, homes, and even churches.

IN PARTICULAR

CATHOLICISM AFFIRMS: It is allowable and proper to have religiously representative objects in public places, homes, and churches.

The very next verse after the "no graven images" verse makes it clear that fabrication of images isn't the problem, but *worshiping them* as gods. "You shall not bow down to them or serve them," the commandment continues, "for I the Lord your God am a jealous God." Later in Scripture, God confirms through Moses what the issue with graven images really is: "You shall make for yourselves no idols and erect no graven image or pillar, and you shall not set up a figured stone in your land, *to bow down to them*; for I am the Lord your God" (Lev. 26:1, emphasis added). As this verse makes more clear, the problem is not the making of these things but making them in order to worship them.

This seems to go without saying for things like pillars (which no Protestant claims should not be allowed in churches!), but because the term *graven image* is so connected to idolatry in the minds of many Christians, it is easy to get them confused. Obviously the problem with graven images is not simply that something is carved or something is erected in a place of worship, but that something is *worshiped in place of* the true God.

Sadly, many Protestants think that Catholics worship statues and so the issue remains. To correct this misunderstanding, first it is helpful to acknowledge that Catholics are very physical worshipers. The Church teaches that human beings are not just souls riding around in "Earth suits" made of meat. Rather, we are embodied rational souls. So if worship is to engage our whole being (as it should), it needs to be physical as well as mental. Because our souls interact with the world through our physical senses, Catholic worship provides input not just for the ears, but for the eyes (and nose!) as well. Hence the use of sacred images and other visual elements like vestments and architecture, along with music, candles, water, incense, and more. Likewise the attention to postures—standing, sitting, and kneeling—and gestures like making the sign of the cross and folding hands in prayer.

But is this truly unique to Catholics? Not in my experience.

Certain elements of Catholic worship are indeed cut out from Protestant services—but they are not missing entirely. It would be odd indeed, for example, never to see a Protestant pray with folded hands and closed eyes. Protestants might laugh at Catholic worship's series of standing/sitting/kneeling, but I've never been to a Protestant church where people didn't sit and stand at least at some points; and kneeling in prayer is not unusual for Protestants outside of church. And I had not been a Christian for more than a few weeks when I discovered that whether or not to hold up hands during worship was a contentious issue for Protestants.

All of this to say that Protestants do recognize that physical actions seem to have spiritual effects. They might not take that principle as far as Catholics, but it's a matter of degree rather than distinction.

IN PRINCIPLE

PROTESTANTS AGREE: Worship of God can involve physical activities that engage the body as well as the mind.

IN PARTICULAR

CATHOLICISM AFFIRMS: Since humans are composites of body and soul, worship rightly includes physical elements that engage the senses.

Even when Protestants agree on the physical aspects of worship, some of the input and action in a Catholic church—like praying before a statue or kissing an icon—can seem too much like idolatrous worship, no matter how much Catholics explain the difference between worshiping an object as God and using an object as an aid to worshiping the one true God. Yet even here there may be some helpful parallels we can use to find accord.

Many Baptist churches feature an American flag behind the area of the church that Catholics would call the sanctuary. Many of the same churches will also lead their congregation in the Pledge of Allegiance during a worship service or sing patriotic hymns like *America the Beautiful.* No one in those churches, however, ever thinks he's being asked to worship the flag or the nation for which it stands.

Neither do Protestants generally have a problem with showing reverence to objects outside a worship setting: for example, by kissing the portrait of a loved one or visiting a deceased relative's gravestone. They don't regard such actions as idolatry or ancestor-worship. They understand that, because we are sensory creatures, we can feel connections to things through representations of them or monuments to them. When we kiss a picture, set up a nativity scene, or hang a banner, we are not confusing those objects with the things they are images of; rather, we use them as points of focus that help us direct our minds to the contemplation of what they stand for. This is nothing like the sin of idolatry in Scripture where the thing made is actually worshiped (c.f. Isa. 44:15).

IN PRINCIPLE

PROTESTANTS AGREE: We can use and interact with objects in ways that promote reverence and remembrance without engaging in worship of them.

IN PARTICULAR

CATHOLICISM AFFIRMS: We can use and interact with objects to promote prayer and to remember God's holy people without being guilty of idolatry.

Knowing Christ and Him Crucified

One Protestant criticism that might surprise Catholics concerns the use of crucifixes. Discomfort with images of Mary or the saints might seem understandable from a Protestant perspective, but how could they complain about an image of our Lord? If worshiping before an image of a cross is acceptable in Protestant services, why not before an image of Jesus on his cross?

A common reason is that some Protestants believe that crucifixes focus undue attention on Christ's death at the expense of his resurrection. "Christ is risen!" they will say—he is no longer on the cross! Of course, Catholics are well aware that Christ is now in heaven, and will point out that to have the image of Jesus suffering on the cross for our sins in no way implies that we deny his resurrection and "keep him dead on the cross." But for some Evangelicals, this is what the crucifix says.

And yet, Protestants do not tend to protest crèche scenes (often in statue form) of Jesus in the manger. Does displaying the baby Jesus in the manger deny that Jesus ever grew up, threatening nearly every doctrine of Christianity? Or for that matter, does the Protestant focus on an empty cross (which is hardly a symbol of resurrection, besides) indicate a denial of Jesus' real suffering and death?

Of course not! And in the same way, the use of crucifixes in devotion or worship does not deny that Jesus was taken down from the cross, was buried, and gloriously rose from the dead.

IN PRINCIPLE

PROTESTANTS AGREE: Images of Jesus Christ from various points in his life and ministry do not deny or downplay other points in his life and ministry.

IN PARTICULAR

CATHOLICISM AFFIRMS: Images of Jesus Christ on the cross do not deny or downplay his resurrection or any other point in his life and ministry.

As we seek accord with Protestants on this point, let us remember that St. Paul included the crucifixion as a key component of the gospel message: "I preached to you the gospel, which you received, in which you stand, by which you are saved, if you hold it fast—unless you believed in vain. . . . that Christ *died for our sins* in accordance with the scriptures, that *he was buried*, that *he was raised* on the third day in accordance with the scriptures, and that *he appeared*" (1 Cor. 15:1–5). In fact, in his ministry Paul chose to focus on the crucifixion, and made a point of telling us so: "When I came to you, brethren, I did not come proclaiming to you the testimony of God in lofty words or wisdom. For

I decided to know nothing among you except Jesus Christ and him crucified" (1 Cor. 2:1–2).

Calling Men "Father"

A common tactic used by Protestants to show that Catholics simply do not follow the Bible is to challenge the Church's practice of referring to bishops and priests as "Father." On the surface, this might seem like a pretty open and shut case. After all, Jesus says, "Call no man your father on earth" (Matt. 23:9). How much clearer could it be?

One of the difficulties here is that other (apparently) equally clear statements of Jesus are not followed literally by any Christians. Protestants use the word *father* to refer to people other than God (for example, their own fathers) and do not get challenged for doing so—and for good reason. For one thing, Scripture itself uses *father* to refer to men besides God. In Jesus' genealogy in Matthew 1, the word is used consistently to refer to mere men. Jesus himself refers to various people as *father* in his Sermon on the Mount (Mark 7). St. Peter refers to the Old Testament patriarchs as *fathers* (Acts 3), as does St. Stephen, the first Christian martyr (Acts 7). Paul refers to *fathers* such as Abraham in his writings (e.g., Romans 4), and St. John addresses one of his epistles to human fathers (1 John 2:13). Thus even from Scripture alone it seems clear that no one could have thought that Jesus meant to prohibit us from using the word for anyone but God.

Another problem with using Matthew 23:9 against Catholics for their use of *father* as a title is a parallel verse in the Gospel of Mark. There, Jesus strongly implies that the word *good* should not be applied to anyone but God (10:18). Yet all Christians—Protestants included—use *good* in descriptions of many people and things besides God. Jesus also said to call no one *teacher* (*rabbi*) (Matt 23:8), yet Protestants use that title with impunity. Some Protestants have even used titles such as *divine* for their own theologians. So they seem not to take such verses literally, as well as to understand that some words may be justly used in reference to God *and* in reference to human beings.

IN PRINCIPLE

PROTESTANTS AGREE: When Jesus said not to call someone father or good or teacher, he didn't mean it as an absolute, literal prohibition in all instances.

IN PARTICULAR

CATHOLICISM AFFIRMS: When Jesus said to call no man father, he did not mean to exclude using the word as a religious title—but rather to remind us that God is our Father in the truest, deepest, and most singular sense.

Vain Repetition

Catholics are often accused of praying in "vain repetition" when saying their prayers (especially the rosary, which is mostly a collection of repeated prayers). This criticism comes from Jesus' words in the Sermon on the Mount in the King James translation of Matthew 6:7 ("But when ye pray, use not vain repetitions"). Because Catholics offer numerous repeated prayers, they are said to violate this command.

Although most Evangelical Protestants do not include many standardized, communal prayers in their worship, nearly all denominations at least pray the Our Father (the "Lord's Prayer") regularly. (Note the irony that the most repeated prayer in Christianity is found in the same passage as the warning against vain repetition in prayer—Matt. 6:7–13!) Even many extemporaneous, "Spirit-led" prayers tend to follow certain patterns of diction, since it's just natural for people to fall into patterns when activities are repeated—especially those done in community where unity is desired. So Protestants can be similarly repetitive when they pray.

There is an ongoing joke in the Protestant world about repeated words and phrases in otherwise spontaneous prayer. I don't know when it started, but the use of the word *just* (as in, "Lord, we just ask you . . .") is ubiquitous in many prayer circles. Even years after becoming Catholic, it is difficult for me to get through a personal prayer without telling God that I "just" ask this and that I "just" ask for that (also!). I knew others who could not seem to transition between sentences without addressing "Father God" each time. We don't talk to each other like this, but for some reason these repetitive words and phrases have worked their way into common Protestant prayer.

Now, there's nothing wrong with that, biblically at least. It's human nature to fall into patterns of speech, even speech directed to God. The real question is whether or not those patterns are helpful or hurtful to worship. That is to say, repetition is not the issue—*vain* repetition is. So what makes repetition "vain"? The biblical word derives from the Greek term *battalogeo,* which means "to babble, speak without thinking"—not just to say the same thing more than once.[37] Modern translations make it clearer what Jesus meant. For example, the Revised Standard Version and the English Standard Version both render the verse as "Do not heap up empty phrases." Other translations use the words *meaningless* (NASB) or *babble* (NIV). The problem, then, is not praying with repetitive words or phrases, but using words that are empty.

Reading the rest of the verse is important here as well—for it indicates what *makes* the repeated words vain. The King James adds, "as the heathen do: for they think that they shall be heard for their much speaking." The "heathen" here are Gentiles (as rendered in most modern translations) who "think that they will be heard for their many words." So what makes the words vain or useless is that they are being repeated for *attention*—not that they are simply said more than once—turning prayer into a cynical, insincere exercise.

We can also note together that this is not Jesus' only admonition about prayer. Just before the verse in question, in fact, he says not to *stand* while praying (Matt. 6:5)—yet both Catholics and Protestants sometimes stand when they pray. Jesus also said to pray alone in a room or closet (Matt. 6:6)—yet neither Catholics nor Protestants limit themselves to these locations for prayer.

Why aren't these verses a problem? Because when we stand to pray or when we venture outside a private space to pray, we aren't doing so *in order to be seen by others* (Matt. 6:5) *or for earthly reward* (Matt. 6:6). Protestants accept such qualifications of our purpose in Matthew 6:5 and 6:6—so why not 6:7?

IN PRINCIPLE

PROTESTANTS AGREE: Prayer may validly involve repetition, standing, or non-private spaces, because Jesus' warnings about such things are to be taken in a qualified sense.

Repeatedly and sincerely telling family members or friends that you love them is not a problem for them, and neither does God tire of hearing our loving prayers even when words are repeated. As for prayers that are vain and meaningless—well, I think we can agree with Protestants that we shouldn't say those even once!

Prayer and the Saints

Even a Protestant who understands that statues aren't idols and that all repetition in prayer isn't bad will often have a more serious issue with Catholics' praying to anyone other than God—typically, those who have departed this life and now reside in heaven (the saints). They may have a number of reasons, but the two big ones are 1) that Scripture forbids contacting the dead, and 2) that it seems that the saints are being worshiped.

The Bible is quite clear that acting as a *medium* (one who facilitates communication between the living and the dead) or practicing *necromancy* (communicating with the dead—often by summoning their spirits) is forbidden (see Deut. 18:9–11; Lev. 19:31; Isa. 8:19–22). Why does Scripture forbid this?

Fortunately, we don't have to guess, since those verses tell us. Deuteronomy 18:9–11 says, "When you come into the land which the LORD your God gives you, *you shall not learn to follow the abominable practices of those nations.* There shall not be found among you anyone who burns his son or his daughter as an offering, anyone who practices divination, a soothsayer, or an augur, or a sorcerer, or a charmer, or a medium, or a wizard, or a necromancer."

Isaiah 8:19 says, "And when they say to you, 'Inquire of the mediums and the necromancers who chirp and mutter,' *should not a people inquire of their God?*"

And Leviticus 19:31 says, "Do not turn to mediums or wizards; do not seek them out, *to be defiled by them*: I am the LORD your God."

In all three examples, summoning spirits is forbidden because it is the way pagans (who do not know the true God) *attempt to gain knowledge they should get from God* (should he wish to give it).

A fascinating story from 1 Samuel highlights this principle. King Saul had prayed to God and received no answer, so he sent for a medium to summon the spirit of the prophet Samuel (ch. 28). The medium does so, and Saul then falls down before Samuel and speaks with him. The important thing to note here is that no judgment is passed for this act.[38] (Imagine the Protestant reaction if this story had been in one of the "apocryphal" books!)

But prayer to saints is not a summoning of the dead—nor is it an attempt to gain arcane knowledge. Rather, it is *requesting that the saints pray for us* to God. Protestants have no problem asking fellow Christians (whom they also consider saints; see 1 Cor. 1:2; Rom. 1:7) to pray for them (see James 5:16; Eph. 6:18), and we know from the Bible that those who are in heaven are not dead but alive (Mark 12:27). Catholics believe that, taken together, these principles practically beg for prayers to the saints!

But can the saints in heaven even hear our prayers?

We may think of heaven, and consequently the saints, as very far away, but the book of Hebrews makes it clear that "we are surrounded by . . . a cloud of witnesses" (dead saints, cf. Heb. 11) and Revelation says that these saints pray to God concerning things going on back on earth (Rev. 5:8, 6:9–11, 8:3–4). And of course, with God all things are possible. So, scripturally, it's not a problem to say that saints can be aware of our prayers and also pray on our behalf.

The picture is completed by James 5:16: "The prayer of a righteous man has great power in its effects." Since the saints in heaven are purified from all sin (1 John 1:7–10, cf. Rev. 21:27), they are perfectly righteous. Shouldn't we *want* them to pray for us? (More on that below.)

IN PRINCIPLE

PROTESTANTS AGREE: Christians on earth should pray for each other and ask for prayers.

IN PARTICULAR

CATHOLICISM AFFIRMS: We can ask Christians in heaven for prayers and they can pray for us.

Even if saints are able to pray for us, for many Protestants there's a more basic problem: prayer should only be directed to God, because it's a form of worship. So praying to a saint always equals idolatry. (This problem is only heightened when Catholics pray such prayers in front of *statues* of saints.) Given the thinking and practices of many Protestants, this is an understandable confusion—but it is a confusion.

To alleviate this confusion, we must begin with the nature of prayer. Although some of the Greek scriptural terms translated into English as "pray" refer only to a request made to God, not all of them do.[39] There are prayers of praise and thanks to God, but there are also "mere" requests (such as are found repeatedly in the Our Father). It is this usage the Catholic has in mind when he speaks of prayer and the saints. Here, "prayer to" is equivalent to "asking of." This is why when saints are invoked in prayer it usually follows the formula "St. X, *pray for us.*" Similar to how the English word *pray* was once used for common requests, when we request that someone else pray for us, we are *praying* that they pray for us! As most Protestants will acknowledge, this sort of request, at least, is biblical (e.g., 2 Thess. 3).

Finally, if you want to get technical, every prayer to a saint *is* a prayer to God! The saints in heaven do not yet have their resurrected bodies, so they can't see us or hear us with their own senses. What they know, they know because God informs their souls directly. Thus, when we ask Mary or any other saint to pray for us, we are asking them *through* praying to God, even if that is not made explicit in our words. So praying to the saints is actually praying through God to the saints that they pray to God for us!

IN PRINCIPLE

PROTESTANTS AGREE: Requests can be made without implying worship, and requesting others to pray for us is biblical.

IN PARTICULAR

CATHOLICISM AFFIRMS: Prayer to the saints is requesting their prayer on our behalf and does not include worship.

Now, most Protestants are familiar with the idea of a prayer request. Often in private or group prayer, participants are asked to share anything they would like other people to pray about for them.

Even making a prayer request of a fellow Christian is a kind of prayer, as we have seen. Protestants make that request (prayer) to their fellow Christians rather than to wicked people or non-believers because they think fellow Christians are more likely to pray for them and because they think the prayers of believers are more effective than those of non-believers. That makes sense. And there are numerous indications in Scripture that prayers to our fellow Christians in heaven would be highly effective.

John tells us that "we know that God does not listen to sinners, and if anyone is a worshiper of God and does his will, God listens to him" (John 9:31). Peter notes that "the eyes of the Lord are upon the righteous, and his ears are open to their prayer" (1 Pet. 3:12). And St. James admonishes us, "Confess your sins to one another, and pray for one another, that you may be healed. The prayer of a righteous man has great power in its effects" (James 5:16).

Now, if we believe that God hears the prayers of righteous believers in an especially effective way, then imagine how powerful the prayers of the saints who are perfected in heaven must be!

As we saw in the book of Revelation, the saints are aware—somehow—of what is going on in the physical world (6:10). Putting all of this together, we can see that there is biblical support for the idea that the saints can know what we are praying, that their prayers for us will be very powerful, and that our request for them to pray for us is itself a form of prayer that is not the same as the worship due to God alone.

IN PRINCIPLE

PROTESTANTS AGREE: The intercessory prayers of other Christians are valuable, powerful, and should be sought.

IN PARTICULAR

CATHOLICISM AFFIRMS: The intercessory prayers of the saints (perfected Christians in heaven) are valuable, powerful, and should be sought.

Language plays a big part in this misunderstanding. Words (like *pray*) evolve along different tracks in different cultures, and their different senses need to be broken down and understood. Sometimes interpreting traditional wording according to modern word usage doesn't work. As we will see next, the same issue also applies to the word *worship*.

Your Worship

A common Protestant criticism of Catholic prayer practices involves the concept of *worship*. Claims vary as to what Catholics allegedly worship or how, but in anti-Catholic polemics it usually does not take long to find accusations of some kind of false worship.

I remember being taught quite clearly, for instance, that Catholics worship Mary.[40] Usually what followed as evidence for this claim were not quotes from Catholic authorities that used the word *worship* but descriptions of pious prayers and activities that Protestants equate with worship.[41] Of course these are two very different claims, and more careful writers admit that the Church does not actually say Mary should be worshiped as God (even if they then assert the opposite based on their own understanding).[42]

Considering the gravity of such a charge, the Church needs to be allowed to speak for itself. Here is what the *Catechism* says of worship: "Adoration and honor given to God, which is the first act of the virtue of religion (2096). Public worship is given to God in the Church by the celebration of the Paschal Mystery of Christ in the liturgy (1067)." This may seem cut and dried, but as is usual in a world of changing linguistic conventions and theological precising over the centuries, the word *worship* has not always been used in this general way.

Like *prayer*, the English word *worship* has a complicated etymological past. It comes from "worth-ship" which simply refers to the condition of being worthy. We note this in older English expressions such as the title "your worship." Simply calling a bishop or king by such a title was (and is) not tantamount to worshiping him as a deity. No one reading Chaucer's *Canterbury Tales* would think that Theseus was an idolater for his "worshipful service" to Arcita! Even in the marriage vows from the Anglican *Book of Common Prayer* we find the line, "With my body I thee worship." But does this track with the biblical term usually translated as "worship"?

In the New Testament the word most commonly translated as worship is *proskuneo*. This word literally means to "kiss toward" but refers to a bow of reverence.[43] It was "used to designate the custom of prostrating oneself before a person and kissing his feet, the hem of his garment, the ground, etc.; the Persians did this in the presence of their deified king, and the Greeks before a divinity or something Holy."[44] This reverence or worship could be paid to mere human beings (e.g., Rev. 3:9) or (far more commonly) to

God (Matt. 4:10; Luke 4:8; etc.). Context, then, determines whether this is what is commonly meant as worship (i.e., toward God alone) or simply respect for a human being.

To *worship*, then, is to assign or recognize a person's "worth"—without specifying what *kind* of person it is or the *degree* of recognition the person is due. This is why the Church is careful to distinguish various levels of "worship" based on the worth of its object. The Church distinguishes these using the Latin theological terms *dulia*, *hyperdulia*, and *latria*.[45] God alone is worthy of ultimate worship (*latria*— which we combine with *idol* to make *idolatry*). This does not mean, however, that no amount of honor ("worthship") is due any other being. We are, for example, supposed to honor our father and mother (Eph. 6:2). *Honor* is a type of "worthship" that the Church calls *dulia*. Veneration of this kind is based on the worthiness of the object of honor and is therefore always less than the worship due to God. Finally, because Mary is the mother of God (because Jesus is God) she is reverenced most highly among all created beings—a "worthship" called *hyperdulia*.

When understood in this manner, it should be clear that so long as the "worthiness" we affirm of someone is accurate, it's not idolatry to assign it to them and act accordingly. Protestants certainly do not disagree that honor or reverence is due to non-divine persons so long as it is proportionate to their worthiness.

PROTESTANTS AGREE: Proper reverence is due even to non-divine persons based on their inherent worthiness.

IN PARTICULAR

CATHOLICISM AFFIRMS: Proper reverence is due to the saints, especially Mary, based on their inherent worthiness.

But doesn't the Catholic practice of bowing before or making other physical gestures of reverence toward saints' statues or relics indicate that they are, indeed, worshiping them? It might seem so, given that at times Scripture describes people bowing down in worship (e.g., 2 Kings 17:35).

Yet even in Scripture this is not always the case. Joseph's brothers bowed to him (Gen. 42:6). A man from the camp of Saul prostrated himself before David (2 Sam. 1:2). King David, a man after God's own heart, "bowed with his face to the ground and prostrated himself" before Saul (1 Sam. 24:8). Moses bowed down and kissed his father-in-law (Exod. 18:7). Women bowed before men (later revealed to be angels) and were not rebuked for it (Luke 24:5). And in Revelation 22:8, John bows to the angels who had shown him the amazing things that God wanted him to know. In fact, he says, "I fell down to worship at the feet of the angel."

From these verses we can see that, according to the Bible that Protestants take as their sole rule of faith, it is not the case that bowing always indicates worship. Bowing or falling at someone's feet are elements that may *accompany* worship, but they are not *identical* with it. So long as bowing indicates proper reverence and not improper worship, there should be no problem.

Catholics reverence the saints because they have been perfected by God and are models of faith for us. This reverence extends to the things those saints have left behind on earth. Whether it be body parts, personal belongings, or just things that have touched these things,[46] Catholics honor objects connected to the earthly lives of the saints. This treatment of saintly relics is pretty much completely alien to Protestantism—but it really shouldn't be.

For one thing, even Protestants may keep (and respect) body parts of their loved ones. My mom has a box of my baby teeth, and my wife and I keep our children's as well. We also have a lock from each of their first haircuts. Most Protestants treat cemeteries as hallowed ground and will visit and pray at the sites where the bodies of their loved ones reside. Some even keep the ashes of their loved ones in special containers that are themselves kept in places of reverence. For most people, none of this is seen as unusual or creepy when it comes to regular people, but for some reason they think it so with relics of the saints.

And the reverential treatment (even sometimes the miraculous power) of relics is found in the Bible. A dead body came back to life when it touched the relics of the prophet Elisha (2 Kings 13:20–21). A woman was cured of hemorrhaging by touching just the hem of Christ's cloak (Matt. 9:20–22). The objects Paul carried with him were used to do "extraordinary miracles" (Acts 19:11–12). Sick people were healed when the mere shadow of the apostle Peter passed over them (Acts 5:14–16). It seems clear, then, that God uses material objects connected to saints in amazing ways.

Historically, there have been numerous reports of healings and other miracles associated with saintly relics. Even the relics themselves may bear traits of the miraculous—such as body parts that do not decay.

IN PRINCIPLE

PROTESTANTS AGREE: Honoring the physical remains of passed loved ones is appropriate, and God uses material things connected with holy people to do great works.

IN PARTICULAR

CATHOLICISM AFFIRMS: Saving and honoring the physical remains of the saints is appropriate, and physical things connected with the saints can be instruments of grace.

Like the use of icons and statues, relics can provide a connection to the saints (and thus God) but at an even more personal level. They are part of the *sacramental* view of the world that most Protestants have forgotten or rejected—but can still rediscover.

The Heart and the Matter

According to the Church, a sacrament is a physical means that God uses to transmit grace. Using physical *matter* and the *form* of words and gestures, they do not simply symbolize or memorialize the grace they represent, but *actualize* it, bring God's life and power to the sacrament's recipient.

Most Protestant churches at least practice baptisms, marriages, and some form of Communion, but they will not usually refer to these activities as sacraments because they do not like the idea that God's grace can be mediated.[47] Without going into the details of every single sacrament, I think it is important to see that there is a larger issue behind them all.

An Anglican priest once said to me that many Protestants embrace a sort of "practical Gnosticism"—referring to the ancient heresy that taught that the *spirit* is inherently good but *matter* is inherently evil. Accordingly, walk into a typical Evangelical church and you'll often see what is essentially a stage that is nearly barren of physical objects or images. The "altar" is typically reduced to a lectern. The worship service is nearly all information-based, with few rituals or other physical actions performed by the clergy or the laity. Sermon topics are often equivalent to Bible studies, and those that focus on conversion are directed at changing one's *mind*—rarely one's actions.[48] In other words, the Protestant faith is defined primarily by our mental thoughts—not our physical actions.[49] Hence "practical Gnosticism."

The Catholic Church recognizes that the spiritual and the material are distinct (otherwise you'd have the opposite error of *monism*), but it doesn't strictly separate them. As we noted before, because human beings are by nature embodied souls, the body is not just the soul's "earth suit."[50] Rather, humans are singular substances with both a material and an immaterial aspect. Because God is the primary cause of all created things, both are good (Gen. 1:31).

In the Old Testament, God regularly used physical objects as a means of accomplishing his will (e.g. the burning bush, Moses' staff, the Ark of the Covenant, etc.). God imbues some physical actions with spiritual effects, such as circumcision and baptism (John 3:5–10; Col. 2:11–12). Christianity itself began with the incarnation of Jesus Christ: the coming-together of God (who is spirit—John 4:24) and human nature (which is physical—Luke 24:39) in a single person (Gnostics reject this belief). This same Jesus was baptized in *water* (Matt. 3), performed a miracle with his *cloak* (Matt. 9:20), and healed with *mud* and *spit* (John 9:6).

God did not have to use physical objects to accomplish his will, but he did—and it is fitting that we, who are material and immaterial beings, should be affected by both matter and spirit. This is what we mean by a "sacramental" view of the world. This interaction between the material and immaterial is not limited to the Church, but it does find its highest expression there. Catholics treat physical objects as able to connect them spiritually to God or others. Not only sacraments but icons, statues, relics, and *sacramentals* (sacred objects that aid prayer and devotion) all flow from this principle.

Certainly, God did not have to make the world this way. He could save without baptism or forgive sins without a priest.[51] He could have appeared as a man on earth without being born of a mother. In fact, he could have redeemed the world without being incarnated into it at all, but merely appearing to us in spiritual forms. But in affirming salvation history and the gospel, Protestants signal at least a basic understanding of the sacramental principle: God working in and through the world. That can be the basis for deeper accord.

PROTESTANTS AGREE: In revealing himself to the world and redeeming it, God chose to work through material agents.

CATHOLICISM AFFIRMS: God continues to use the material agents of the sacraments to bring grace to the world.

Not only in their theology but in their regular practice it seems clear that most Protestants have not fully rejected such a worldview. Who among them would empty their coffee into a baptismal font? Would any Protestant not be incensed by someone spitting on their wedding ring? Can we imagine a Protestant tossing a Communion cracker into the air and catching it on his tongue for comedic relief? No—they grasp that there is something to these physical objects that goes beyond their material, or else they would mean nothing more than dishwater, minerals, or snacks.

Even Protestant groups that do not consider ordination a sacrament will often recognize a distinction between clergy and laity. It is common practice for pastors to baptize even though technically anyone could perform the rite. It is rare for Christian couples to marry without an ordained minister. Pastors are often given a high place of honor even though they may not have any more theological training than the person in the pew.

Perhaps this is all so, they might reply—but any grace that comes through physical objects or through human ministers is God's and not man's! Yet this is exactly what the Church teaches about the sacraments. Their operation is entirely the work of God, independent of the holiness of the minister or the recipient.[52] This is why the Church teaches that priests can forgive sins and effect transubstantiation even when they themselves lack personal faith or holiness.

That the sacraments do not rely on men for their success sometimes gives rise to an opposite sort of objection from Protestants, especially those who object to infant baptism because babies cannot yet express their own faith. If babies can be baptized without yet being able to confess Jesus as their savior, it seems to turn God's grace into a magic trick.

Yet we see the sacramental in a parallel action in the Old Testament, where faithful Hebrews were to have their babies circumcised on the eighth day of their lives (Gen. 17). This brought them into communion with the people of God long before they had the ability to make such a choice. Although covenant faithfulness was required of those wanting to remain part of God's people (e.g., Lev. 26:14–39; Jer. 3:8), those lacking the ability to demonstrate it could still become full members. In much the same way that Americans are born into citizenship without their initial consent but later remain citizens by choice, God counts the faithfulness of a baby's parents toward his salvation until such time as he attains the age of reason and can be held responsible for his decisions.

St. Paul himself makes the connection between circumcision and baptism, in Colossians chapter 2. Regardless of what is made of that connection, the fact that physical actions mattered to God *whether personal faith was involved or not* is clear from Israel's example—and most Protestant denominations agree that baptism functions in the same way for Christians as circumcision did for Israelites.

PROTESTANTS AGREE: Becoming part of the people of God through a physical action does not always require personal faith.

CATHOLICISM AFFIRMS: Becoming part of the people of God through baptism does not always require personal faith.

Hocus-Pocus

The Catholic sacrament that Protestants most often dismiss as "magic" is the Eucharist—the belief that by the words of a priest, a piece of bread can be made into the real body of Christ while retaining the physical characteristics of bread, and wine can be made into the real blood of Christ while retaining the characteristics of wine. In fact, the magical phrase *hocus-pocus* is commonly thought to derive from mockery of the Latin for "this is my body," which the priest says over the Communion host (*hoc est corpus meum*).

For example, one Protestant scholar writes, "It is idolatrous to worship the host. . . . this is a form of idolatry. For it is the worship of something which the God-given senses of every normal human being inform them is a finite creation of God, namely, bread and wine. It is to worship God under a physical image which is clearly forbidden in the Ten Commandments (Exod. 20:4)."[53] Another calls belief in the Eucharist "not literalism, however, but fantasy."[54] The charge of "hocus pocus" seems to make sense if one agrees that, "the mass shows absolutely no evidence of being a miracle."[55]

What is interesting about this attitude is that the non-sensual basis for belief in the Eucharist is exactly what one would expect if the dogma were true. This is because the consecrated host does *not* change in sensible ways (and *non-sensed* does not equate to *nonsense!*). To understand this clearly, we need to discuss the teaching of transubstantiation.

Around the thirteenth century, the word *transubstantiation* came to be used to help explain what the Church believed from the beginning about the real presence of Christ in Holy Communion,[56] when St. Thomas Aquinas applied Aristotle's philosophical terms to deepen our understanding of the mystery. Aristotle distinguished between what something *is* (*substance*) and non-essential characteristics of that thing (*accidents*). An accident can alter a substance without changing its nature.

For example, when a child grows up, he gets taller but remains the same person. So growing tall would be called an *accidental* change—likewise, dyeing one's hair or losing a limb. But when a change occurs that changes what something actually is—like a tree being cut down and becoming a pile of firewood—that is known as a *substantial* change.

Now, because humans only perceive the accidents of a substance, we can't recognize substantial change unless we also see the accidental changes that ordinarily accompany it. But the miracle of transubstantiation is that God changes the elements of bread and wine into the body and blood of Christ without any accidental change. Therefore, everything that the senses perceived about the elements remain the same even though by faith we can know they *are* no longer what they were.

Protestants may deny or even scoff at this explanation. It should seem somewhat familiar to them, though, since the doctrine of Christ's divinity, which all Christians profess, is based on a similar principle. To the senses of those who knew him on earth, Jesus looked nothing like the infinite God! He had the appearance of a human; he ate, drank, slept, bled, and died like a human. The Incarnation can only be seen through the "eyes of faith," and the same is true of the Eucharist.

It's not a perfect comparison, since Christ is both God and man, whereas the Eucharist has ceased to be bread and wine and is only Christ's body and blood. (The belief, held by some Protestants, that somehow *both* bread/body and wine/blood are present, is called *consubstantiation*.) The body that was (and remains) part of Jesus' human nature is not a mere appearance. But the comparison does serve to show how Protestants readily profess—as a core doctrine—something that was never apparent to the senses.

The same thing can be said for all the sacraments, really. Baptism may only *appear* to make somebody wet, yet according to Scripture it brings with it the power of salvation (John 3:5; Acts 2:38; 1 Pet. 3:21). A person may not look any different after being confirmed (Acts 8:14–17; Heb. 6:2) or married (Gen. 2:24; Mark 10:9) or ordained (1 Tim. 5:22) —yet they really are different in some significant way. The same can be said for a person who has undergone initial justification, and Protestants would agree that such a person is actually very different from what he was. There are no visible signs when you're "born again," but they believe it happens.

IN PRINCIPLE

PROTESTANTS AGREE: A spiritual reality can be quite different from physical appearances or lack thereof.

CATHOLICISM AFFIRMS: The Eucharist only appears to be bread and wine, but it is actually Jesus' flesh and blood.

It is interesting to note that although virtually all Evangelicals deny the reality of sacraments, almost across the board they practice some of them or rites similar to them. Nearly all Protestants baptize, and nearly all practice Communion or the Lord's Supper. All celebrate marriage. Many believe it is helpful to call in their pastor for special prayer when they are sick, and even in Baptist circles, which have done away with infant baptism, they often have "baby dedication" services that closely mirror aspects of infant baptism. Pentecostals believe that even after baptism the Holy Spirit must be received in a special way (as in confirmation). The ordination of Protestant ministers is often quite ceremonial. Thus, although they usually deny that any actual sacramental grace comes from these actions, they still seem to find it important to practice them.

Earlier we noted that God doesn't *have* to work through sacraments. Why do we think he chooses to? There are a range of fascinating possibilities for why God has chosen the sacraments as his normative means to communicate grace, but none of them will satisfy the person asking if the question originates in doubt. In revelation God does not give a specific reason for why he has chosen to partner with the physical things in his creation (including its people) in his work. However, we know that he does so—and the sacraments are, in a sense, the least interesting examples.

During Jesus' ministry he performed numerous miracles. He raised Lazarus from the dead simply by calling to him, and he raised the centurion's servant from the dead from a long distance away apparently without doing anything. One time, a woman was miraculously healed simply by touching Jesus' robe. Jesus rarely performed miracles in the same way more than once, though on at least three occasions he healed somebody using his spittle (Mark 7:33, 8:23).

Whatever God's reason for working within creation—to show its value, to catch people's attention, to validate certain contemporary ideas, or for some other reason, what we know for sure is that it shows that God wills to cooperate with his creation in his saving work. This is a point on which Catholics and Protestants can build significant accord.

Catholic worship often looks odd—perhaps even blasphemous—to many Protestants. In the end, however, much of this discomfort comes from misunderstanding the intent or thinking behind the disagreeable actions. When Protestant principles are applied to Catholic particulars, a different story often emerges. Many of the elements of Catholic worship that Protestants object to are perfectly acceptable when seen in the same way that many Protestant practices are understood.

As we will see next, this is true even with one of the most difficult topics for Protestants to accept: the doctrines and practices concerning the Blessed Virgin Mary.

4

Mary and the Saints

When it comes to Catholic teachings that make Protestants uncomfortable, it would be difficult to find one that does a better job than the veneration that Catholics show to Mary. The discomfort arises on more than one level, beginning with the idea that she or anyone else in heaven can hear us at all. As we saw in the last chapter, even if the saints can hear us, to many Protestants it's blasphemous to pray to them. After all, isn't Jesus the only mediator between God and man (1 Tim. 2:5)? Finally, even if there is some sense in which prayer to the saints is acceptable, they think that the flowery and pious-sounding words used to praise Mary, in particular, simply do not seem justified.

In theology, certain positions are based not merely on direct scriptural or traditional support but on the conclusions arrived at from more basic theological conclusions. As we will see, much of what the Catholic Church teaches with regard to Mary and the saints is based on theological conclusions that are not themselves unacceptable to Protestants.

Intercessors and Mediators

We have seen that both Catholics and Protestants are okay with the idea of someone praying for them and that because the saints in heaven are alive, it makes sense to ask for their prayers. All the more, then, do Catholics see asking Mary (saint *par excellence*) for prayer as proper (as have some Protestants[57]).

It is important to note that anyone who does so is by definition an *intercessor*. Using this word should also not be a problem for Protestants, because St. Paul uses it when he instructs Timothy, "First of all, then, I urge that supplications, prayers, intercessions, and thanksgivings be made for all men" (1 Tim. 2:1). Yes, in the book of Hebrews, Jesus himself is referred to as an intercessor (7:25), but this doesn't mean that no one else can be. The *kind* of intercession Jesus performs is unique, but intercession itself is not limited to his work (even if other kinds are dependent on it).

The same can be said of the word *mediator*. A mediator is simply one who stands in the middle between two parties (see Gal. 3:19–20). When it comes to understanding the mediatorial role of the saints, we must understand *what is being mediated*, not simply point to the use of that particular word. So although many Protestants object when the Church refers to the saints or Mary as mediators, since 1 Timothy 2:5 says that "there is one mediator between God and men, the man Christ Jesus," we aren't forced to conclude that the Church sees Mary and the saints as usurping Christ's singular mediatorial role. As with intercession, mediation can take different forms depending on what is being mediated and who is doing the mediating.

We are not left to guess what kind of a mediator Jesus is—we are told quite clearly that Jesus is the mediator *of the New Covenant* (Heb. 8:1–6, 9:15, 12:24). So 1 Timothy 2:5 is not saying that there can be no mediation of any kind other than that of Jesus; it is saying that Jesus alone mediates the New Covenant.

Although it might seem that roles ascribed to Jesus must, by their very nature, always be completely unique, a quick perusal of the Bible indicates that this is not the case. Scripture says that Jesus is the "builder" (Matt. 16:18), yet so are other Christians (1 Cor. 3:10). Jesus is the "living stone" (1 Pet. 2:4), and so are his followers (1 Pet. 2:5). Jesus is the "light of the world" (John 9:5), and we are to be the light of the world as well (Matt. 5:14). Jesus Christ is the foundation stone of the Church (1 Cor. 3:11), but the Church is built on the foundation of the apostles and prophets (Eph. 2:19–20).

In none of these examples do Protestants object to the Bible's presentation of titles or roles being shared between Jesus and others. Evangelical scholar Ron Rhodes makes this distinction clear in a book written to address the errors of cults: "Jesus is the ultimate Light of the world (Matt. 4:16; John 8:12; 1 John 1:7). Believers are lights only in a derivative sense, as we are reflective of his light."[58] Likewise, in his introduction to the New Testament, Donald Guthrie notes that St. Peter "thinks of Christians as living stones. And because this spiritual edifice consists of living people, he identifies them as a living priesthood. But the thought of living stones leads his mind to dwell on Christ, the chief corner-stone."[59] In his writings, W.E. Vine recorded, "God is said to be the builder, in 1 Corinthians 3:9; Christ in Matthew 16:18; Paul in Romans 15:20, cp. 1 Corinthians 3:10; 2 Corinthians 10:8; 13:10; the "gifts" of the ascended Lord are the builders in Ephesians 4:12, cp. 1 Corinthians 14:12; individual believers, here; and in Ephesians 4:16 the church is said to build itself up in love."[60]

IN PRINCIPLE

PROTESTANTS AGREE: Scriptural titles and roles ascribed to Jesus can be shared with or ascribed to others as well.

IN PARTICULAR

CATHOLICISM AFFIRMS: The scriptural titles and role of intercessor and mediator ascribed to Jesus can be ascribed to or shared with others, including Mary and the saints.

As with the word *prayer*, the argument over *mediator* is an example of why Catholics and Protestants need to learn to speak each other's language before judging each other. There can be a similar semantic breakdown when it comes to the language of veneration that is sometimes directed to Mary or other saints. It must be admitted that at times Church writers have used quite flowery language to express their devotion to Mary especially. Even the words of the Hail Mary prayer, though biblical and fairly innocuous compared with some devotional writings, can sound downright blasphemous to some Protestants. Why is Mary being "hailed"? Why is she being called "holy"? To many Protestants, those words sound like they should only be directed to God.

Sometimes the language used in prayers to Mary or the saints is so effusive that appealing to the ways that language changes over time isn't enough. The *Salve Regina* prayer, for example, calls Mary "our life, our sweetness, and our hope." Surely, many Protestants think this kind of language crosses the border into idolatry.

But these same Protestants can also understand how we sometimes use over-the-top terms when speaking of someone we love—especially someone in our family. Now, we know from Scripture that it is appropriate to see God as our Father, and many Protestants are comfortable concluding from this that Jesus is our brother. Likewise, they view other Christians as their brothers and sisters in Christ.

Catholics take these family ties very seriously and don't hesitate to use loving language in reference to our brothers and sisters in heaven: the saints. We also extend that analogy to Mary, receiving her as our own mother just as Christ commanded from the cross when he said to Mary, "Woman, behold, your son!" and then to the beloved disciple, "Behold, your mother!" (John 19:26–27).

No one would begrudge another person the effusive words of love he uses toward his mother. If I thanked my mother for "giving me life," few Evangelical theologians would intervene to remind me that it was actually *God* who gave me life. No one would criticize a child for giving his dad a shirt that says, *"Best Dad in the World!"* because it is not literally true. We all recognize exaggerated expressions of love and know how to put them in context. Devotional language used for Mary or the saints is likewise the poetic, hyperbolic language of love—not the language of systematic theology.

Such romantic exaggeration is employed in the Bible as well. Jacob told his brother Esau that "truly to see your face is like seeing the face of God" (Gen. 33:10). Cities with high walls are said to be built "up to heaven" (Deut. 1:28). When David killed Goliath, he was praised for killing tens of thousands of Israel's enemies (1 Sam. 18:6–8). A woman praised King David with the words, "My lord the king is like the angel of God" (2 Sam. 14:17). Are we to believe that the entire "world" followed Jesus during his ministry (John 12:19)? And how many Christians have amputated body parts that were used to sin (Matt. 18:8–9)? Hyperbole and other poetic writing forms are not unknown in Scripture, and they are not unknown in the Church's later writings either.

IN PRINCIPLE

PROTESTANTS AGREE: It can be appropriate to use flowery or hyperbolic language when expressing love or making a poetic point.

IN PARTICULAR

CATHOLICISM AFFIRMS: It's appropriate to use exaggerated and poetic words when expressing love for our mother Mary and our brothers and sisters the saints.

Maddening Marian Doctrines

Protestants often take issue not just with Catholic prayers to Mary but Catholic teachings about her—especially the four main or *de fide* Marian dogmas. First among those teachings is the doctrine of the Immaculate Conception—the belief that Mary was preserved from original sin from the moment of her conception and did not commit sin during her life. Part of the issue is that it seems to conflict with verses like Romans 3:23, which says that "all have sinned and fall short of the glory of God."

Although Paul's words in Romans 3 may sound like an open and shut case, no orthodox Protestant actually believes that the word *all* here refers to every human being who has ever lived.

Jesus Christ (whom the verse does not specifically exclude) was fully human, after all, and yet was without sin. Many Protestants also believe that infants and those with diminished mental capacity do not or cannot commit sin. So if Protestants admit of at least some exceptions to Romans 3:23, it's inconsistent to object to the Immaculate Conception by treating this verse as an absolute proof that every human, *ever*, has sinned.

Romans 3:23 is not the only example in Scripture where "all people" clearly does not refer to every single member of a given group. The apostle Matthew says of John the Baptist that "all Judea and all the region about the Jordan were going out to him, and they were baptized by him in the river Jordan, confessing their sins" (Matt. 3:5–6). In John 8:2, it says that when Jesus came to the temple, "All the people came to him, and he sat down and taught them." In Acts 22:15, the apostle Paul was said to be "a witness for him to all men." In these examples and many others (e.g., Matt. 10:22; 21:26; 2 Cor. 3:2; Rom. 16:19; Acts 21:28; 2 Tim. 3:9; 3 John 1:12), most Protestants would not hold to a literal, exception-less interpretation of *all*.

IN PRINCIPLE

PROTESTANTS AGREE: Not every single human who ever lived committed sin, and in Scripture, the phrase "all people" or "all men" is not always to be interpreted strictly literally.

IN PARTICULAR

CATHOLICISM AFFIRMS: Romans 3:23 does not prove that Mary couldn't have been free of original and personal sin.

Another issue that is sometimes brought up concerns the *reason* for Mary's immaculate conception. If Mary had to be sinless in order for Jesus to be born sinless, it is argued, then wouldn't Mary's *mother* also have to be sinless? The problem with this question is that it implies something that the Church does not teach—namely, that Mary *had* to be sinless in order for Jesus to be born sinless. God certainly could have caused Jesus to be conceived and borne in the womb of a sinful mother. For that matter, he could have made the Incarnation happen with no mother at all! But he saw fit to have Jesus be incarnated in the womb of a mother and for that mother to be sinless.

In the Old Testament, the Ark of the Covenant carried the Ten Commandments, which represented the presence of God on earth. Accordingly, it was considered so pure that even to touch it carried a death sentence (2 Sam. 6:6-7). In the New Testament, God's presence is incarnated in Jesus, the God-man who, as an unborn baby, was carried in the womb of Mary. Christian tradition views the ark as a *type* or forerunner of Mary, and just as it was fitting (though not strictly necessary, since God can do anything) for God's presence in the Old Testament to be borne inside a pure vessel, so was it fitting for God incarnate to be borne inside a woman untouched in any way by sin.

It is important to note that the Immaculate Conception doesn't imply that Mary was not in need of a savior (see Luke 1:47). The merits of Christ's saving work on the cross were applied to Mary, too—just immediately upon her conception and not later on. God saved Mary from sin in the same way that we save clothes from getting dirty by keeping them out of the mud in the first place instead of washing them after they have fallen in. Surely God is not limited to applying his saving grace in only one way.

Protestants believe that Jesus was conceived without sin, but he is not the only one. Both Adam and Eve were created without sin as well. Being sinful, then, is not essential to human nature; rather, it is the consequence of the fall and affects those who go through the ordinary process of being conceived and born into humanity. But that doesn't preclude God, for whom all things are possible, from acting in an extraordinary way as part of his plan for salvation.

IN PRINCIPLE

PROTESTANTS AGREE: God can work outside his normative ways of doing things, even when it comes to salvation.

IN PARTICULAR

CATHOLICISM AFFIRMS: God uniquely applied Jesus' saving grace to Mary before she was born.

Mary's divine maternity is the second doctrine. You might think that referring to Mary as the "mother of God" should not be upsetting to any Protestant who understands the Incarnation, which was defined at the Council of Chalcedon in 451. (Mary was called "mother of God" even earlier, at the Council of Ephesus in 431.) Yet there are some who believe the title to be indicative of errant Catholic teaching. Since divinity is eternal and has now a mother, they say, we should just refer to Mary as the "mother of Jesus' humanity."

Protestants agree that in the Trinity there are three persons who each possess the nature of God. Protestants further agree that in the Incarnation, one of those persons (God the Son) took on an *additional* nature—that of humanity. Now, in the early days of the Church there were numerous attempts made to hammer out exactly what these truths entailed.

By the fifth century, the Church had defined that Jesus took on the nature of humanity but this did not result in there being an additional *person*. His two natures were united in and through his one person. This means that when something is said about Jesus Christ in either his humanity or his divinity, it refers to the one divine person. Thus we can rightly say, with Martin Luther for example, that "God in his own nature cannot die; but now, since God and man are united in one person, the death of the man with whom God is one thing or person is justly called the death of God."[61]

Now, mothers do not give birth to natures—they give birth to persons. Because Jesus is God, a divine person, Mary is rightly called the mother of God. And we can rightly say that God was conceived and was born in a manger, even though divinity never has a birthday![62]

So we see that referring to Mary as the mother of God is not some exaggerated title that the Catholic Church invented to make Mary seem more special than she actually is. In fact, recognizing her as the mother of God is arguably less about honoring her and more about affirming the orthodox doctrine of the Incarnation defined by the early Church, and all its implications.[63]

IN PRINCIPLE

PROTESTANTS AGREE: Mary is truly Jesus' mother, and because Jesus is one person who is both truly God and truly man, what is affirmed of him is rightly affirmed of God.

CATHOLICISM AFFIRMS: Mary, as the mother of Jesus who is God incarnate, is the mother of God.

Ever Virgin

The Church has taught from early times that Mary was a virgin not just before Jesus' conception but for the rest of her life. Most Protestants say that Scripture doesn't teach this and in fact contradicts it—making the whole idea a "tradition of men" that exalts Mary beyond what she deserves.

Now, it is true that Mary's perpetual virginity is not spelled out in Scripture. Neither, however, is it asserted she did *not* remain a virgin after Jesus' birth. But Protestants conclude that she did not remain a virgin based on a) the fact of her marriage to St. Joseph, b) the Bible's reference to Jesus' "brothers and sisters" (e.g., Matt. 13:55; Mark 6:3), and c) Matthew 1:25, which says that Joseph did not have relations with Mary "until" she had given birth to Jesus.

It's true that marriage ordinarily involves sexual relations. But then, when your child is the son of God, that makes your marriage "extraordinary" by any definition! And in biblical times, marriage did not require consummation to be ratified. In fact, Church tradition holds that Joseph took Mary to be his wife even though she was a consecrated virgin—which explains Mary's response of disbelief when the angel Gabriel told her she would conceive and bear a son (Luke 1:34). The *Protoevangelium of James,* a document written around A.D. 150, says that Joseph was an elderly widower who took Mary as his spouse to guard and protect her—including her vow of virginity. Although this document is not inspired

Scripture, its teaching reflects a common belief among the early Christians.

This helps explain why, when St. Joseph was considering divorcing Mary quietly, he was told not to be afraid "to take Mary your wife" (Matt. 1:20). This would not make sense if Joseph and Mary were not already considered married apart from sharing sexual relations.[64] Even if this was not a common practice, Protestants acknowledge that God often calls people to unusual life circumstances when they are to be used in unusual ways—such as when God commanded Hosea to marry a prostitute (Hos. 1:2).

This also helps us understand Mary's confusion about Gabriel's message at the Annunciation. When she is told that she would conceive and bear a son, she responds with disbelief (Luke 1:34). This is a rather odd response, since Mary must have known that having children ordinarily went with marriage. It seems that when she told Gabriel, "I do not know a man,"[65] she not only saw herself as a virgin presently but also in the future—*even though she was betrothed to Joseph*. But if she had been a consecrated virgin, her expression of confusion would make sense. She knew she would *never* have sexual relations, and so she didn't think she would ever conceive and bear a child.[66]

What about Jesus' "brothers and sisters"? None of his "brothers" are ever actually said to be Mary's son even though Jesus is (John 2:1; Acts 1:14). Furthermore, the Greek words often translated as *brother* or *sister* have a much wider range of meaning than first-degree siblings. Sometimes they refer to more-distant blood relations like cousins or even just fellow-believers in Christ (e.g., Gen. 13:8; 1 Cor. 15:6). Because these terms have multiple possible definitions, context must always determine their meaning.[67] So the Bible doesn't force us to conclude that Mary had other natural children after Jesus (which helps explain why Martin Luther,[68] John Calvin,[69] and Ulrich Zwingli,[70] all affirmed Mary's perpetual virginity).

A final difficulty often cited by those who hold to Joseph and Mary's eventual sexual relations is the word *until*. In the Gospel of Matthew we are told that Joseph "took his wife, but knew her not until she had borne a son" (Matt. 1:24–25). Does this mean that the holy couple only refrained from sexual intimacy until Jesus was born? The text doesn't tell us either way.

Despite what some commenters have said, the Greek term translated "until" (*heos*) does not have a singular meaning any more than it does in English. It can denote the end of a period of time (e.g., "up until") or contemporaneousness (e.g., "as long as" or "while").[71] Therefore, saying that something did not occur *until* a certain time may mean simply that it didn't occur up to that time, with no implication of what happened after, or it could imply that the thing did happen subsequently.

We come across this ambiguous use of *until* elsewhere in Scripture, and typically let context help us interpret it. For example, Paul tells Timothy to "attend to the public reading of Scripture, to preaching, to teaching" until he comes (1 Tim. 4:13). Certainly Paul did not want Timothy to cease these practices after he arrived.[72] Or consider Michal, daughter of Saul, who "had no child to [*heos*] the day of her death (2 Sam. 6:23)!

That even Martin Luther[73] and John Calvin, architects of the Reformation, agree with the Church here[74] is certainly one area for building possible accord. But there's another.

As a former Evangelical and now a Catholic apologist, I would say that the perpetual virginity of Mary is easier to defend than some other things that most Christians—Protestants included—take for granted in Scripture. Skeptics have made careers out of poking holes in the history of the

Gospels, for instance, pointing out inconsistencies they believe cannot be harmonized. They try to debunk miracles, or even disprove Jesus' very existence.

In response, Protestant apologists use logic, original-language arguments, historical facts not asserted in Scripture, and other traditions to support what they believe are orthodox, biblical Christian teachings. They know that skeptical, superficial readings of the Bible often do not turn up the full truth. If they applied that same thinking to the perpetual virginity of Mary, they might come to see it in a new light.

IN PRINCIPLE

PROTESTANTS AGREE: Sometimes it takes a wide range of interpretive tools to understand the meaning of Scripture verses—including those on Mary's virginity.

IN PARTICULAR

CATHOLICISM AFFIRMS: Biblical data about Mary, properly understood, do not disprove her perpetual virginity but can in fact support it.

Assumed into Heaven

Another area of disagreement with a core Marian doctrine concerns the end of Mary's earthly life and thereafter: the belief, befitting her holiness and God's will that the vessel that held the God-man should not experience decay, that she was assumed into heaven at the end of life.

Protestants object to the dogma of Mary's assumption into heaven primarily because it is not recorded in Scripture.

But this is not a positive disproof; after all, we are not given details about how many New Testament figures met their end. Even the historical treatise of the book of Acts ends with Paul in prison and does not record his final missionary journey to Spain nor his death at the hands of Nero. In fact, even though only one of the apostles' deaths is recorded in Scripture (that of St. James the greater), Protestants regularly affirm the traditions concerning their deaths.[75] It should not come as a surprise, then, that we do not have details of the end of Mary's life.

Apart from the silence of Scripture, Protestants should not have any difficulty in believing in at least the *possibility* of Mary's assumption, because she is not the first person to have traveled to heaven at the end of her life. (Note that the Church has not definitively said whether "end of her life" refers to Mary being assumed while still alive or upon her natural death.) Both Enoch and Elijah were said to have been taken up into heaven prior to their death (Gen. 5:24; 2 Kings 2:11), and Protestants affirm these accounts without reservation.

IN PRINCIPLE

PROTESTANTS AGREE: We can believe traditions about the fate of New Testament figures even when they're not recorded in Scripture, and there is no biblical problem with God assuming someone into heaven.

IN PARTICULAR

CATHOLICISM AFFIRMS: Mary was assumed into heaven at the end of her earthly life even though it is not recorded in Scripture.

Queen of Heaven

Continuing with our somewhat chronological look at Marian doctrines, the Church teaches that after Mary's assumption, she was given a regal position of honor and power: "crowned queen of heaven." For many Protestants, this teaching proves that the Church has truly gone off the rails! Isn't this title taken from pagan religions?[76] Wouldn't it mean that Mary is God the Father's wife? Doesn't it make Mary part of the Trinity?[77]

Although these kinds of questions are somewhat understandable based on a modern, Western conception of royalty, they do not account for the biblical culture on which the title and doctrine are based.

We know from Sacred Scripture that in Israel, the king's *mother* was given the title of queen (e.g., 1 Kings 15:13, Jer. 13:18, 29:2; 2 Kings 24:15; 10:13). Jesus, of course, sits not only on the Davidic throne (Luke 1:32), but he is seated on the throne of heaven (Heb. 1:8–9, 4:16). He is indeed the king of kings (1 Tim. 6:15; Rev. 17:14)! Thus, following from the practices of the culture into which he was born, Jesus' mother would be considered a queen. Like everything that makes Mary special, her queenship is a reflection of her son's glory.

Protestants, of course, are typically happy to recognize Jesus' supreme kingship (sometimes they do this better than Catholics!), and they try to see the world through biblical paradigms. Thus they should be ready to understand how Mary's queenship makes perfect sense.

IN PRINCIPLE

PROTESTANTS AGREE: Jesus is a king, Mary is Jesus' mother, and according to Jewish reckoning in the Bible, the mother of a king is a queen.

MARY AND THE SAINTS

IN PARTICULAR

CATHOLICISM AFFIRMS: Jesus' mother Mary is queen of the whole domain of which Jesus is king.

Of course, Jesus is not the king of an Old Testament nation under the Old Covenant, so it may seem a stretch to apply the title of queen to Mary. However, this is not the only piece of biblical evidence we have for its application. In the book of Revelation we read about a woman "clothed with the sun, with the moon under her feet, and on her head a crown of twelve stars" (12:1). So here we have a woman in the heavens (or heaven—see verse 7) wearing a crown (a pretty good indication that she is a queen)—but who is she? We are told in verse five: "She brought forth a male child, one who is to rule all the nations with a rod of iron, but her child was caught up to God and to his throne." This male child who rules with a rod of iron is clearly Jesus (see Rev. 2:27). Doing the math, the woman must be Mary.

Now, there are other possible interpretations of this passage. Some of the descriptions of the woman suggest she is a symbol, perhaps of Israel—cf. 12:6. However, it would be a false dilemma to limit the interpretation either to one or the other. Protestants generally understand that scriptural figures can be multivalent. They regularly make claims about Jesus' role as Messiah based on Israel's history and culture, for instance, and they discover types and figures of Jesus in the Old Testament. They don't force strict either/or interpretations in these cases, and neither does the Church in these passages from Revelation.

The same goes for the accusation that "queen of heaven" is a pagan title, stemming from its use in the biblical book of Jeremiah to refer to the Assyrian/Babylonian goddess named *Ishtar* or *Ashtoreth* (7:18, 44:17–25). If it means one thing in one part of the Bible, they assume that has to be its only meaning.

Of course, it is also true that the Hebrew word for *God* was also used of pagan false gods. Even Jesus' title *king of kings* was used in the book of Daniel to refer to a pagan king (2:37). But of course no Protestant balks at either term because of these pagan associations. They know that titles and words in Scripture are often used in more than one way, and context indicates which meanings are appropriate.[78]

IN PRINCIPLE

PROTESTANTS AGREE: Scriptural figures and titles can have more than one meaning or application.

IN PARTICULAR

CATHOLICISM AFFIRMS: The woman in revelation can symbolize Mary and other figures, the use of *queen of heaven* in Jeremiah does not taint its application to Mary.

Mary Appears

After her assumption into—and crowning in—heaven, Mary's activity did not cease. The Church has investigated and approved (though not defined as part of the Faith) reports that Mary has appeared and delivered messages in various times and places all over the world. To many Protestants this sounds incredible, but the fact is that some of these miraculous apparitions have more witnesses than did Jesus' own resurrection.

One of the best-attested appearances occurred in Fatima, Portugal in 1917. Three children claimed to have seen Mary in the field while tending their sheep. This continued for six months, with Mary giving the children various messages. The children's testimony was not well received in the village, however, and so Mary made a final appearance on October 13 that is now known as the miracle of the sun. Reports say that an estimated 70,000 people were in attendance and saw the sun "dance in the sky."[79] Given that many Protestant apologists point to the few hundred eyewitnesses of Jesus' resurrection as proof of its historicity, such a confirmation of a Marian apparition would seem to carry even more force.

It should also not be a theological problem for Protestants to accept that Mary could have appeared after her death. Bible-believing Protestants already accept that Moses, Samuel, and Elijah appeared in the land of the living after their earthly life had ended (1 Sam. 28; Matt. 17)—and with fewer witnesses than some of these Marian appearances. It's one of the miraculous "tools" that God uses to deliver messages to his people. Thus, it seems that neither history nor theology stands in the way of reaching accord on the possibility of Marian apparitions.

IN PRINCIPLE

PROTESTANTS AGREE: Saints can appear on earth after they have died, and historical evidence can prove when it occurs.

IN PARTICULAR

CATHOLICISM AFFIRMS: Several of Mary's appearances have been historically attested-to by sound evidence.

What the Church teaches about Mary is not as contradictory to or unsupported by Scripture as many Protestants have been led to assume. Further, the historical and theological principles that undergird the Church's teachings cohere with the kinds of methods Protestants use to support Christian doctrines that they affirm. Even in this area, often considered one of the biggest stumbling blocks for Protestants investigating Catholic belief, we can see that there are many built-in points of agreement that can serve as foundations for greater accord.

5

Sin and Morality

There is an idea among some Protestants that all sin is equal. Although tacitly recognizing that certain sinful actions are morally worse than others, they seem to get hung up on the idea that any sin is imperfection and any imperfection will keep someone out of heaven (this is why Jesus—who is perfect—must stand in our place). If this is the case, then any sin will send someone to hell, so any distinctions in gravity among sins is pointless. Therefore, all sin is equal. Sometimes they will quote St. James, who writes, "Whoever keeps the whole law but fails in one point has become guilty of all of it" (James 2:10).

Now, common sense tells us otherwise. A Hyundai and a Lamborghini are both cars, but they are clearly not equal! All broken laws are broken laws, and anyone who breaks the law is a lawbreaker no matter which law he broke. That does not, however, mean that there is no hierarchy within the law. Indeed, it seems evident from numerous passages of Scripture that various sins can result in varying levels of punishment. Jesus tells the Pharisees that they will receive a greater condemnation for their actions (Mark 12:40). He tells his disciples that anyone who will not listen to what they say will be judged more harshly than Sodom and Gomorrah (Matt. 10:14–15). James warns teachers that they will be judged more severely than others (James 3:1). St. Peter says that for those who have come to the knowledge of Jesus Christ but then again defile themselves with the world, it would have been better if they had never known the way of righteousness (2 Pet. 2:20–22). John records Jesus saying that Judas has a greater sin than Pilate (John 19:11).

We perceive a similar hierarchy when it comes to good works. Several times in the Sermon on the Mount, Jesus says that certain actions will lead to greater rewards (e.g., Matt. 5:11–12, 6:1–6, 16–20). How is it that these greater rewards are gained? Jesus said it's according to what people do (Matt. 16:27). This concept is illustrated in the parable of the talents (Matt. 25:14–30) and repeated by Paul in Romans 2:5–6: "He will render to every man according to his works." Paul also distinguishes between the reward received by those whose good works endure and those whose do not: "If the work which any man has built on the foundation survives, he will receive a reward. If any man's work is burned up, he will suffer loss, though he himself will be saved" (1 Cor. 3:14–15; cf. Rev. 20:12).

But although many Protestants typically shy away from assigning salvation-merit to good works or damnation-judgment to evil works, many agree there is indication that these very things are taught in Scripture. Evangelical apologist Norman Geisler, for example, lists degrees of happiness in heaven and punishment in hell as an area of agreement between Catholics and Evangelical Protestants: "As to the degree of punishment, Roman Catholicism holds that 'The punishment of the damned is proportioned to each one's guilt.' Augustine taught that, 'in their wretchedness, the lot of some of the damned will be more tolerable than that of others.' Just as there are levels of blessedness in heaven, there are degrees of wretchedness in hell."[80]

IN PRINCIPLE

PROTESTANTS AGREE: Moral common sense and Scripture teach that not all sins are equivalent.

IN PARTICULAR

CATHOLICISM AFFIRMS: Sins are not equivalent—either in seriousness or their effects on salvation.

Now, because most Protestants have an essential commitment to the idea that our good works play little to no role in our (ultimate) salvation due to their affirmation of *sola fide,* there seems to be a similar commitment to the idea that our bad works (sins) contribute nothing to the salvation equation either. This has the effect of flattening out the relative moral status of sinful acts, contrary to the Catholic Church's distinction between mortal and venial sin.

According to the Church, there are some sins that, though violating the moral law, nevertheless do not destroy the relationship a person has with God. Other sins, however, bring so much harm to our relationship to God that it effects separation. The former are known as *venial* sins, the latter *mortal* (meaning deadly to the soul; damning). This idea that some sins are not only worse than others, but are so much worse that they merit their own category, does not always sit well with the Protestant ethos.[81]

What may seem curious about Protestant reticence to accept this distinction is that it is unambiguously defined in Scripture: "If anyone sees his brother committing what is not a mortal sin, he will ask, and God will give him life for those whose sin is not mortal. There is a sin which is mortal; I do not say that one is to pray for that. All wrongdoing is sin, but there is sin which is not mortal" (1 John 5:16–17). Because many Protestants believe that *every* sin is mortal in the sense that it makes the sinner deserving of hell (even if they will go to heaven because of their faith in Jesus), they see this passage as a warning against loss of faith (apostasy)—not simply a particularly grave sin.[82]

So, although most Protestants affirm directly or indirectly that some sins are worse than others and that in some way they affect salvation, where the disagreement usually lies is with the *stage of salvation* that these various works affect (we'll discuss this more in chapter 7). However, whether they affect salvation or damnation one way or another, that they have an effect seems clear, even by Protestant principles.

IN PRINCIPLE

PROTESTANTS AGREE: Peoples' works—good or bad—affect their salvation or damnation in some way.

IN PARTICULAR

CATHOLICISM AFFIRMS: Peoples' works increase or decrease the grace of salvation in various ways.

Once Saved, Always Saved?

Another important feature of the Church's teaching on salvation is that the reward of salvation can be lost. Here it takes its cue from Scripture.

St. John, writing to Christians, says that we must follow God's commandments and that if we do so, we will "not lose what you have worked for, but may win a full reward" (2 John 6–8). James explains that people can both wander from the truth and be brought to it, resulting in salvation (James 5:19–20). Similarly, Paul stresses endurance in the faith (1 Cor. 15:2; Gal. 6:8–9; 2 Tim. 2:12), as does the book of Hebrews (6:4–6, 10:26). These epistles reflect the teaching of Jesus, who said that "he who endures to the end will be saved (Matt. 10:22). Paul adds that God is "severe" to those who have fallen, and that if we do not continue in his kindness, we will be cut off (Rom. 11:22).

Now, a host of prooftexts can likewise be marshaled that seem to indicate that salvation will never be lost (e.g., John 10:28; Rom. 8:38–39, 11:29; 1 John 5:13), and many Protestants profess belief in this "eternal security." However, even many of those who hold to this theological position still will not express complete confidence that they are one of the redeemed because the only way to be sure is never to fall away!

We are all aware of people who seemed to show every sign of true faith but later fell away from it. Protestants typically come down into one of two camps in explaining this phenomenon. On the more "Calvinist" side, salvation is an act of God that cannot fail, and so no one can "unsave" himself any more than he can save himself. Therefore, anyone who falls away from the faith was never truly saved in the first place. For those on the "Arminian" side, salvation is more of a cooperative act, and God will allow those who freely believed (resulting in their salvation) to freely disbelieve (resulting in damnation). This means that those who fall away really might have been on their way to heaven but then ceased to be.

But whether the fallen-away really were saved and then lost their salvation through sin or unbelief or were never "really" saved in the first place, at the end of the day almost everyone agrees that falling away is possible.

PROTESTANTS AGREE: People who show every indication of having been Christians may not be saved.

IN PARTICULAR

CATHOLICISM AFFIRMS: People can actually fall away from the faith, lose sanctifying grace, and be damned.

When it comes to our works (good and bad) a similar line is drawn. For those in the Calvinist category, works are strongly indicative of salvation. It has been said that if Jesus is not the Lord *of all* then he isn't Lord *at all*. In Protestant circles this is known as "Lordship Salvation."[83] Contrary to this position is that of the "Free Grace" group.[84] Free Grace so emphasizes God's unilateral bestowal of saving grace that one's works (good or bad) become effectively moot. However, even in this paradigm, works have great effect on the reward one receives in the afterlife. In both cases, our works (whether good or bad) have an effect on our salvation.

IN PRINCIPLE

PROTESTANTS AGREE: Our works (whether good or bad) have at least some effect on our salvation.

IN PARTICULAR

CATHOLICISM AFFIRMS: Our works (whether good or bad) seriously affect our salvation.

Finding a satisfactory way to affirm the truth of all Scripture verses on salvation topics is not an easy task. The different ways Protestants have sought to resolve the tension created between these various passages has resulted in denominational splits and endless debates. Protestants may not agree with the Catholic resolution to these passages, but then again they don't agree among themselves, either! By beginning with the scriptural distinction between mortal and venial sins and with the universal perception that some people do apparently lose their faith, we can all strive for accord on these important questions of salvation.

Counting Our Sins

Another difficulty the Protestants often have with Catholic teaching is on what counts as sin in the first place. Protestant reliance on Scripture for morality, while often rightly considered a virtue, can be a kind of vice if it excludes other sources of guidance on good and evil. Because the Catholic Church believes that all truth is God's truth, what we are able to learn from God's revelation in nature, through observation and reason, is also authoritative, and must cohere with his revelation in Scripture. This is what we call the *natural law.*

Briefly, natural law derives moral principles from creation (i.e., nature). Paul tells us in the opening chapters of Romans that God's nature itself can be known by looking at his creation: "What can be known about God is plain to them, because God has shown it to them. Ever since the creation of the world his invisible nature, namely, his eternal power and deity, has been clearly perceived in the things that have been made" (Rom. 1:19–20). Further, this God has also given all people a moral code that is revealed in nature itself: "What the law requires is written on their hearts, while their conscience also bears witness and their conflicting thoughts accuse or perhaps excuse them" (Rom. 2:15).

How has this been explained by the Church? First, we can discover these things philosophically. By looking at what a thing is, what it is for, and what contributes to its fulfilling its purpose, we can know what is good for it. A good knife, for example, will be sharp. A good shoe, however will be comfortable rather than sharp. We know this because we can tell what a knife or a shoe is for by what it does. When it comes to judging actions, the same method applies. We can tell what an action is and what it is for by what it will naturally accomplish if successful. In cases of morality, if an intentional action supports the good of the actor or subject of the action then it is moral—and if it detracts, then it is immoral. This approach was famously adapted from Aristotle by St. Thomas Aquinas, who said that the natural law is our participation, by our reason, in the *eternal law* that resides in God.[85]

One reason moral law arguments are so important is that they transcend any particular religious revelation. All people are bound under the precepts of natural moral law regardless of what the positive doctrines of their religion tell them. Neither a Christian, Muslim, Buddhist, nor atheist may commit murder, rape, or theft and will be morally culpable if he does—because the immorality of these acts is naturally evident, not positively revealed (though sometimes it's both).

Another reason why the moral law is vital to Christians is that it helps us to interpret Scripture. God's *natural* revelation can help us to understand his *supernatural* revelation. For a revealed moral code to work, it needs more than a list of laws. There are far more acts a person can commit than there are positive commandments in Scripture! So we also need *principles* that harmonize with those laws and allow us to apply them beyond their mere letter. The moral law that God reveals in nature helps us do this.

For example, we might all know that murder is wrong—but is abortion murder? The Bible doesn't say.[86] The Church has been strongly opposed to abortion from its inception.[87] Yet I remember my mentor in Evangelical seminary telling me that he had argued both for and against abortion (under certain circumstances) in two editions of the same book! His knowledge of the Bible did not change from one edition to the next (indeed, he cited many of the same Scripture verses in both arguments), nor did his interpretive strategy. Rather, what changed was his view of abortion. He had never approved of murder and knew the Bible did not either. However, once his understanding of natural law grew, his application of that biblical principle changed.

Because natural revelation is available to all people regardless of religious tradition, it can be a source for reasoning from Scripture toward greater accord. Although it seems that practically any Bible verse can be misinterpreted or misapplied by itself (as the shifting moral codes within the various Christian denominations all too clearly demonstrate), when God's natural revelation is recognized it can serve to stop the slide down the slippery slope of faulty exegesis.

There have been and remain some Protestant scholars who acknowledge and value the natural law. Martin Luther King, Jr. wrote about it famously and eloquently in his *Letter from a Birmingham Jail*. But many Evangelicals today look upon natural law philosophy with skepticism, and that has led to interpretations of the positive, revealed moral law (in the Bible) that vary wildly across the board. There are Protestants who bomb abortion clinics and others who bless them. Entire books have been written on various Protestant views of divorce and remarriage. Some Protestants are radical pacifists, others are eager for war. Some Protestants relegate all homosexuals to hell, while others celebrate their unions and even ordain them to the highest levels of ministry.

IN PRINCIPLE

PROTESTANTS AGREE: In practice, Protestants appeal to extrabiblical reasons for moral guidance and to help interpret scriptural moral precepts.

IN PARTICULAR

CATHOLICISM AFFIRMS: Human reason teaches us moral truths and helps us interpret what Scripture says about right and wrong.

One area where the divide between Catholic morality and Protestant morality—and among the moral teachings of different Protestant groups—has grown is sexual morality. Although in Scripture the Church sees hints of its teaching on contraception (e.g., the story of the sin of Onan in Genesis 38), a strong case against contraception would be difficult to marshal using Bible prooftexts alone. And yet, from the Reformation up till 1930, when the Church of England decided to permit contraception, the vast majority of Protestants, too, opposed it. It must be asked: if the teaching against contraception is non-scriptural, then why was it the Protestant position for over 400 years?

In contrast to this shift in thinking from the Protestants, the Catholic Church remained committed to its anti-contraception position. At roughly the same time that Protestant denominations around the world were switching their positions, the Church was affirming the traditional teaching: in the 1930 encyclical *Casti Connubii* and most pointedly in the 1968 encyclical *Humanae Vitae*. In that document, written at the height of the Sexual Revolution and shortly after the popularization of the birth control pill, Pope Paul VI warned of evils that would follow if contraception became widely accepted. He predicted an increase in marital infidelity, a general lowering of moral standards, a loss of respect for women, and that governments would eventually coerce people into using contraception. That his predictions were correct is a matter of historical record.

Why does the Church take such a strong stand against something that is not clearly spelled out in Scripture? In *Humanae Vitae,* Paul VI stressed that the stand comes from a "reflection on the principles of the moral teaching on marriage—a teaching which is based on the natural law as illuminated and enriched by divine revelation" (4). Indeed, the document contains not fewer than thirty-eight references to nature and nature's laws. Because the Church has deeply reflected upon God's instruction in both creation *and* divine revelation it can justify and continue to hold to the historic Christian position.

When we look at conservative Protestant teachings on life issues such as abortion or euthanasia, it becomes clear that although most may not affirm the connection between abortion and contraception (or divorce, or homosexuality), many are in line with the Church's conclusions on the sanctity of life. Some (unfortunately not all) Protestants have even fought the good fight side by side with Catholics for the end of abortion in America.

Catholics and Protestants affirm that, without grace, mankind is lost in sin. Due to original sin, all are born without the grace required to become saints. Even after receiving such grace, the actions we choose can lead us closer to God or farther away from him. It is even possible that having first received his grace, we could act in ways that sever us from him completely. Though Protestants have some problems with Catholic categories in this area, in practice they evince principles to which Catholics can appeal in a quest for greater accord.

When it comes to Christian morality, the Protestant appeal to Scripture alone has produced a wide range of opinions and practices, some of which reject not only Catholic teaching but historic Protestant teaching. Although the darkness of our sinful intellects and wills certainly is to blame for this ongoing problem, the Protestant rejection of natural law has made it worse, opening the door to debates that should have no traction among Christians.

This is not to say that there are no debates concerning these issues among Catholics! But whereas Catholics who reject the Church's clear moral teachings are dissenters, Protestants can be faithful adherents to the teachings of their own denomination or tradition while flatly contradicting the teachings of another group. And even Protestants who challenge their own group's dogmas can say that they're acting in line with the Protestant principle of private interpretation.

That said, the memory of traditional Christian morality hasn't been extinguished from Protestantism, and neither has the law of God that is written on our hearts. Many Protestants today are dismayed by the retreat from traditional morality, especially sexual morality, and are open to anything that will help strengthen it—even something outside of Scripture. This, too, is an opportunity to build accord and share the riches of the Church's natural law tradition.

As we will see in the next chapter, the Church teaches that the sinful condition in which the world wallows has a solution. Catholics and Protestants alike affirm that God's grace is offered freely to all—including those who lack the ability to know.

6

Salvation and Purgatory

The Protestant Reformation was launched when a Catholic priest named Martin Luther thought he'd discovered something in the Bible that the Church had been missing for centuries. That discovery was *salvation by faith alone*—that is, apart from doing good works. This core Reformation doctrine of *sola fide* is a major dividing line between Catholics and Protestants.

Just like *sola scriptura,* this doctrine ends up dividing Protestants from each other just as much (and sometimes even more) as it divides them from Catholics. Over the years, "faith alone" has come to mean different things to different Protestants. There are some (known as *Free Grace* Protestants) who have taken the principle so far that they believe even apostates can be completely confident in their salvation. At the other end of the spectrum are legalistic or Fundamentalist groups that, while giving lip service to salvation by faith alone, nevertheless demand a severe lifestyle from their members.

Nor is the debate over salvation by faith alone limited to extreme fringe groups. In fact, it began in the sixteenth century and shows no signs of letting up in the twenty-first. A recent book from one of the most popular Evangelical publishers devoted over 300 pages to an academic debate between five scholars on the nature of justification (one was a Catholic).[88]

And justification is only the beginning. Similar debate books have been written about sanctification, pluralism, eternal security, law and gospel, and other related topics.[89] And so as we seek accord, in this chapter we will look to see if the principles that allow Protestants who disagree over salvation nonetheless to identify with one another and to worship together might call for the embrace of Catholics as well.

Are You Saved?

Although Christians sometimes think of salvation in fairly simple terms (going to heaven instead of hell), anyone who spends much time thinking or talking about the subject will quickly discover that there are numerous shades of meaning.

Nearly all Christians, even those who speak of salvation as if it occurred whole and entire at a single point in time, with no potential to ever be lost, recognize that God's work in people typically involves a *process* that is extended over time. In the Evangelical tradition that I came from, we thought of salvation in three basic stages: 1) *justification,* which was the point at which someone received Jesus Christ as his Lord and Savior and thus was guaranteed heaven, 2) *sanctification,* which was the process by which God transformed the individual's life from one of sin to sainthood, and 3) *glorification,* which was the final, complete transformation into perfection that occurred once someone entered eternal life in heaven.

Although this threefold process is described differently among Protestant traditions, most affirm something like it. A critical feature of this theology is that during each stage, the *causes of* and *effects on* one's salvation can differ. For example, whereas the initial stage of salvation ("justification") might be considered a one-way act of God based on faith alone, resulting in heaven or hell, the second stage ("sanctification") may rely heavily on the actions of the individual and only affect one's *degree* of reward or punishment.

The importance of these salvation "stages" is that although Protestants will often speak of salvation as a single moment in time with everlasting effects, most agree that there is more to the story. *Sola fide,* in most Protestant minds, refers only to one's initial justification. This happens to coincide nicely with the Catholic view of baptism—it is entirely faith-based, distinct from a person's works, and instantly brings us into a saving relationship with God.

For many Protestants, the parallels break down after that because the Church teaches that saving grace can be lost or increased via works ("faith working through love" per Galatians 5:6)—but there are Protestants who teach something similar to this as well.[90] In the end, the differences sometimes come down more to terminology and fine-grained distinctions than to entirely different salvation plans as is often believed.

IN PRINCIPLE

PROTESTANTS AGREE: Salvation is in some sense a process involving various stages, each with different requirements and effects.

IN PARTICULAR

CATHOLICISM AFFIRMS: Salvation is an ongoing process with different requirements at different stages that can increase, decrease, eradicate, or regain God's saving grace in our lives.

It's important to note that any one of these three stages can be referred to as "salvation" in a certain context. Some have put it this way: "I *was* saved, I *am being* saved, I *will be* saved." Speaking this way can be a little confusing, though, so theologians typically give these stages their own scriptural label.

Interestingly, although these labels are often taken from biblical terminology, they are not always used in the biblical sense. That doesn't mean that these Protestants are being unbiblical; just that theology is often more precise than the Scripture it is meant to explain. The biblical authors were not writing within a context of long-standing, immutable theological vocabulary. Indeed, with the New Covenant came many new words and new uses of old words.

If we do a Bible word study on terms such as *justification, sanctification,* and even *salvation,* we find that these terms rarely track with their modern usage in theology texts. For example, justification is described in Scripture as being a *past* event (Rom. 4:2–3 and 5:1) but also as a *future* hope (Rom. 2:13, 6:16; Gal. 5:5). Sanctification, too, indicates a *past* occurrence (1 Cor. 6:11; Heb. 10:10, 29), a *present* process (Rom. 6:1–13; 1 Thess. 4:1–3; 2 Thess. 2:13), as well as a *future* promise (Eph. 5:25; 1 Thess. 5:23).

The effect of all this is that when people from different religious traditions converse, they can easily misunderstand

each other. Catholics, for example, typically refer to the salvation process as *justification*. That is, they use it in the same
way that Protestants often use *salvation* when they are speaking generically of all three stages. You can imagine the confusion that can result if one Christian is using a term to refer
to a three-stage process but another is using the same word
to refer to only one of those stages!

A Protestant who is committed to the idea that justification occurs at a single point in time and can never be lost
might sound arrogant to a Catholic who thinks he is talking
about justification as a lifelong process: "How can this Protestant know everything that will happen in the future?"
Conversely, the Catholic who is speaking of justification
as a process might sound very legalistic to the Protestant:
"How can this Catholic say that God saved him because of
his good works?" Between the different definitions attrib-
uted to these precise theological terms in Scripture, and the
fact that they are used differently between different Christian traditions, confusion is not only common but should
be expected.

Although this distinction between justification and sanctification can be helpful in understanding Protestant doctrine,
we should remember that it's a recent development in the
Christian world. In his comparison of Catholic and Evangelical theology, Norman Geisler notes that "Luther also
believed in a progressive sense of the word 'justification.'"[91]
Protestant scholar Alister McGrath, who wrote a defini-
tive volume on the subject of the doctrine of justification,
emphasizes that "neither Martin Luther nor Huldrych
Zwingli understood justification in precisely this manner."[92]
Nonetheless, although he did not flesh out the modern distinction, Luther's thinking laid the groundwork, introducing
"a decisive break with the western theological tradition."[93]

IN PRINCIPLE

PROTESTANTS AGREE: Scriptural terminology often has a wider range of meaning than it does in more precise theological usage.

IN PARTICULAR

CATHOLICISM AFFIRMS: Salvation terminology has a wider range of meaning in Scripture than it does in more precise theological usage.

Who Then Can Be Saved?

Despite these confusions, some Protestant views of salvation actually track pretty well with what the Catholic Church has taught for thousands of years. Very briefly summarized, the Catholic Church teaches that the initial stage of salvation (what many Protestants refer to as *justification*) is accomplished by God's grace alone.

Wait, what?

You read that correctly! Consider these words from the Council of Trent (the council specifically called to address Reformation theology):

And whereas the apostle saith, that man is justified by faith and freely, those words are to be understood in that sense which the perpetual consent of the Catholic Church hath held and expressed; to wit, that we are therefore said to be justified by faith, because faith is the beginning of human salvation, the foundation, and the root of all justification; without which it is impossible to please God, and to come unto the fellowship of his sons: but we are therefore said to be justified freely, because that none of those things which precede justification-whether faith or works-merit the grace itself of justification. For, if it be a grace, it is not now by works, otherwise, as the same apostle says, grace is no more grace.[94]

You will notice that not only is the Catholic position not that we are justified by works (the common accusation), but we are also not (initially) justified by faith. This might sound blasphemous to Protestant ears, but although the phrase "justified by faith" does appear in Romans 5:1, this is not the only relationship that Paul poses between the two terms.

Consider that one of the most popular prooftexts for *sola fide* does not actually say "faith alone" anywhere in the passage: "For by grace you have been saved through faith. And this is not your own doing; it is the gift of God, not a result of works, so that no one may boast" (Ephesians 2:8–9, ESV). I have seen more than one Protestant surprised to reread that verse and realize that if an "alone" is implied in the passage, it's referring to God's *grace*—not a person's faith.

The way the Church has parsed all this out is to say that initial justification is essentially a one-directional action of God whereby he applies his grace to the life of a person even prior to the person coming to personal faith. What follows this initial justification is an ongoing process of justification (what some Protestants would refer to as *sanctification*) that is dependent on the individual's personal faith and the works of love that follow from it (Gal. 5:6). This "ongoing justification" is completed at the time of the individual's death, and bears its full fruit after the general resurrection (the stage some Protestants refer to as *glorification*). Reformed Scripture scholar Guy Prentiss Waters compares justification and sanctification with an alphabetical mnemonic:

- Act: "Justification is an *act* of God. It does not describe the way that God inwardly renews and changes a person. It is, rather, a legal declaration in which God pardons the sinner of all his sins . . . at the very moment that the sinner puts his trust in Jesus Christ."

- Basis: "We are not justified by our own works; we are justified solely on the basis of Christ's work on our behalf."

- Confession: "Sinners are justified through faith alone when they *confess* their trust in Christ. We are not justified because of any good that we have done, are doing, or will do."

- Demonstration: "No one may consider himself to be a justified person unless he sees in his life the fruit and evidence of justifying faith; that is, good works."[95]

In contrast to the above description of the justification salvation stage, Waters states that "sanctification is God's renewing and transforming our whole persons—our minds, wills, affections, and behaviors. . . . [sanctification] is an ongoing and progressive work in our lives. Although every believer is brought out once and for all from bondage to sin, we are not immediately made perfect. We will not be completely freed from sin until we receive our resurrection bodies at the last day."[96]

It is interesting to compare this fairly standard Protestant understanding of salvation with Trent's declaration concerning justification. On the subject of sanctification, the same council goes on to say,

Having, therefore, been thus justified, and made the friends and domestics of God, advancing from virtue to virtue, they are renewed, as the apostle says, day by day; that is, by mortifying the members of their own flesh, and by presenting them as instruments of justice unto sanctification, they, through the observance of the commandments of God and of the Church, faith cooperating with good works, increase in that justice which they have received through the grace of Christ, and are still further justified, as it is written; he that is just, let him be justified still; and again, Be not afraid to be justified even to death; and also, Do you see that by works a man is justified, and not by faith only. And this increase of justification holy Church begs, when she prays, "Give unto us, O Lord, increase of faith, hope, and charity."[97]

In quoting at length from these two opposing theological camps, we can see that in many aspects they may be closer than is often thought (especially once we allow for differences of expression). The same can be said for Lutheran theology, which remains even closer to its Catholic roots than Reformed theology.[98] The journey to accord may be easier than expected if we can better learn how to read each other's maps!

Work with Me Here

The word *cooperate* means to "operate together." If you and I move a couch together, we are cooperating because we are both contributing to the same single goal. When it comes to salvation, a key question then, is whether or not people cooperate with God in the attainment of that goal.

Here it is difficult to discuss "the" Protestant position because there is a larger variance between Protestants on the extreme ends of the salvation spectrum than there is between Protestants and the Catholic Church. However, the two biggest problems that Protestants on either end of the spectrum will have with Catholic soteriology both have to do with cooperation. On the one hand, many Protestants will deny that God ever saves people apart from their own personal faith. Others, notably Calvinists, will not allow the idea that a person cooperates with God toward his salvation in *any* way initially but only in good works after justification takes hold.

No orthodox Christian may affirm that salvation can be earned through a person's good works. (The Reformers made that clear when they cut themselves off from the Catholic Church, and the Church made it clear when it responded at the Council of Trent.) All orthodox Christians must instead affirm that salvation is by God's grace. (The Catholic Church has always taught this, and Protestants affirmed it with another doctrine referred to as *sola gratia*.)[99] So far, so good. Where we run into trouble is the intersection of faith and works and how those relate to God's grace.

In the Protestant world we can contrast two primary positions. First there is what is usually called *Calvinism* (named after the Protestant Reformer John Calvin). For the Calvinist, people's intellects and wills are so totally depraved by sin that they basically lack the ability to contribute anything to their own salvation. God's sovereignty is the singular controlling factor for all salvation dogma. The only way a person can get saved in this system is for God to commit a completely gratuitous act of grace and lift the person out of this state prior to any movement on the person's part. Only after this special act of grace is the sinner's cooperation in the salvation process possible. Because salvation begins with God's justifying action, it cannot fail (and hence cannot be lost). It also cannot fail to produce cooperative good works in the life of the believer—therefore the two should always be found together.

Faith, for the Calvinist, begins as God's action *on* a person—not the free act *of* a person. Good works are a secondary result (and a necessary component) of true faith. Even though works contribute nothing to a person's *justification*, they are impactful to his *sanctification*. Cooperation between God and man is thus the result of salvation, not its cause.

An opposing Protestant position, which we referenced earlier as Free Grace, borrows from Calvinism (especially with regard to the inability to lose one's salvation), but differs in its view of the role of faith and works. In Free Grace theology, a person's faith is something he freely chooses—it is not a cooperative act of God.[100] After justification, not only are good works unnecessary to *attain* salvation, faith itself is unnecessary to *remain* saved. Faith, in the Free Grace system, has so much causal force that its effects can remain even when the cause ceases to exist. Cooperation with any saving work of God is unnecessary for anything but greater rewards in heaven.

Even though these two positions seem to be polar opposites, both sides have collected an impressive arsenal of scriptural prooftexts and theological arguments to support their opposing conclusions.[101] This results in competing theologies that depend for their support on a narrow selection of seemingly clear biblical prooftexts (because *sola scriptura*), and a reinterpretation of those that do not endorse the position.

Given that such divergent views can exist side by side within Protestantism, it seems inconsistent to make too much of similar disagreements between Catholics and (some) Protestants on (some) of these issues. If Calvinist and Free Grace Protestants remain Christian brothers despite these differences, how can they simultaneously judge the Catholic Church (which sits somewhere between these two views) as preaching a false gospel? If accord is to be reached, we must be consistent in our treatment of one another's theological positions.

IN PRINCIPLE

PROTESTANTS AGREE: The relationship between faith and works is complicated, and true Christians can have differing views.

IN PARTICULAR

CATHOLICISM AFFIRMS: The precise relationship between faith and works remains a mysterious cooperation between God and man—one that requires careful handling between both Catholic and Protestant Christians.

Lending God a Hand?

Catholic theology embraces God's sovereignty, his infinite power and omniscience, his self-existence, and a host of other attributes that together paint a picture of a God who is in absolutely no way dependent upon his creation. The Church further affirms that God endowed humanity with the powers of intellect and will. *Intellect* is the faculty by which truth is known, and the *will* is that which always seeks some kind of good and is free to choose it.

Finally, the Church teaches that God, in his grace and mercy and without need or compulsion of any kind, has gratuitously included the free actions of his creatures in the working-out of his will. This means that human free will can be a legitimate cause of action that has God as its ultimate cause. It's not merely instrumental causation, the way a paintbrush is part of the cause of a painting. We're not simply puppets or tools. Rather, when we human beings exercise our free will, we become a secondary cause of an action of which God is the primary cause. His sovereignty and our freedom work together.

And when God promises something on the basis of a person's actions, the Church calls that *merit*. Thus our good actions do not "earn" our salvation as something due to us, but they do bring about the fulfilment of God's promised salvation.

There are numerous examples from Scripture showing that God's sovereignty is not diminished simply because he includes others in the working-out of his will. In fact, Scripture itself is a good example. Paul says, "All Scripture is inspired by God" (2 Tim. 3:16), and Peter explains that "no prophecy ever came by the impulse of man, but men moved by the Holy Spirit spoke from God" (2 Pet. 1:21). Now, God certainly needed no man to create the Bible. He could have simply willed the Bible into existence, whole and complete, and delivered it to his apostles without their ever having to lift a pen—as Mormons believe about their scripture. Or he could have dictated it word-for-word to a human secretary, as Muslims believe about the Quran. But instead he cooperated with human agents, *inspiring* them to write his revelation using their words and means.

Within the pages of Scripture, we read time and time again of God using people to effect his will although it was unnecessary for him to do so. God did not need Moses to pray to save the Hebrews from judgment (Num. 11:1–3). God did not need Mary for his son to be made man (Luke 1:26–38). And Jesus did not need to ascend to heaven and leave behind the Church as his body to continue his work (1 Cor. 12:27; Eph. 4:15–16; Col. 1:24; etc.). It would be easy to go on, but the point should be clear. God, in his sovereignty, chooses to cooperate with man in his work of salvation. He wills that the free wills of his creatures be part of his causal process. How exactly this works out is a mystery, but it is not contradictory.[102]

Protestants recognize these cooperative actions as examples of God's power. Evangelical scholar John Hannah says of Moses' actions in the defeat of the Amalekites (Exod. 17:11–13), "Moses' holding the staff of God (cf. Exod. 4:20) above his head with both hands symbolized Israel's total dependence on the power of God. When Moses lowered his hands, a picture of lack of dependence, the enemy was winning."[103] Note that although God is given all the glory for Israel's victory, it was in some sense dependent on Moses keeping his staff in the air. As Hannah demonstrates, this recognition in no way gives undue credit to Moses—it merely demonstrates that God sometimes works with/through his creation even though it is unnecessary for him to do so.

Surprisingly, the Bible even suggests cooperative action between God and Satan. Baptist theologian Thomas Howe explains how it is that 2 Samuel 24:1 can "claim that God moved David to number Israel when 1 Chronicles 21:1 claims that it was Satan." Howe replies that, "Although it was Satan who immediately incited David, ultimately it was God who permitted Satan to carry out this provocation. Although it was Satan's design to destroy David and the people of God, it was God's purpose to humble David and the people and teach them a valuable spiritual lesson." Howe notes similar situations with Job and even the crucifixion of Christ, which "both God and Satan are involved in . . . Satan's purpose was to destroy the Son of God (John 13:2; 1 Cor. 2:8). God's purpose was to redeem humankind by the death of his Son (Acts 2:14–39)."[104]

A similar idea is present in Scripture with regard to damnation. Moses reports that Pharaoh's heart was hardened by God (Exod. 7:3) but also that Pharaoh hardened his own heart (Exod. 7:13–14, 8:15). Evangelical scholar Edwin A. Blum notes that Israel suffered a similar fate: "People in Jesus' day, like those in Isaiah's day, refused to believe. They "would not believe" (John 12:37); therefore they could not believe (v. 39)."[105]

We can see that Protestants are comfortable with assigning seemingly singular acts to both God and man, or even God and Satan. Even when only one party is given credit (or blame) for a given action, both are acknowledged as part of the cause.

IN PRINCIPLE

PROTESTANTS AGREE: God is sovereign and has no need of his creation's cooperation to accomplish his will, but he often uses it anyway.

IN PARTICULAR

CATHOLICISM AFFIRMS: It pleases God to accomplish his will through the cooperation of his creation.

To be more specific, the Catholic Church holds that God acts to save us in some ways that don't include our free cooperation and in other ways that do. When it comes to the initial stage of salvation (what many Protestants, remember, refer to as *justification*), God acts prior to, and independently of, the free will of the recipient of his grace.

This may sound strange to those Protestants who believe that personal faith is necessary for salvation—for example, that faith must precede baptism—but most Protestants practice infant baptism. For those who object on the basis that God cannot save apart from faith, there is evidence from Scripture that this is not always the case.

We read in the Gospel of Mark that the friends of a paralytic brought him to see Jesus. Because the house was so crowded, they carried him up to the roof, made a hole in it, and lowered him on a pallet down to where Jesus could see him. If personal faith were required for every case of salvation, then what happened next would not be possible: "And when Jesus saw their faith, he said to the paralytic, 'My son, your sins are forgiven'" (Mark 2:5). Scripture makes it clear that Jesus forgave the paralytic based on the *faith of his friends*. Evangelical commentator John D. Grassmick writes concerning this passage that "Jesus viewed the determined effort of the four as visible evidence of their faith in his power to heal this man. . . . and healing was predicated on God's forgiveness (e.g., 2 Chron. 7:14; Ps. 41:4, 103:3, 147:3; Isa. 19:22, 38:16–17; Jer. 3:22; Hosea 14:4)."[106] There are hints of similar occurrences in the book of Acts, where whole households were said to be saved although the faith of only one member is recorded (e.g., Acts 16:15, 31).[107] One explanation for this is that although God requires faith from those with the ability to exercise it, he can dispense his saving grace based on the faith of others, especially for those helpless to exercise it themselves.

PROTESTANTS AGREE: God can dispense his grace based on the faith of others.

CATHOLICISM AFFIRMS: God can dispense his saving grace to people based on the faith of others, especially when they are unable to express faith themselves.

Such a theology of salvation might sound foreign to modern-day Baptists, but it would not have to first-century Jews. Since the time of the patriarch Abraham, faithful Jews had circumcised their children shortly after they were born. This brought them into full membership as God's people, Israel. Paul makes this very parallel between circumcision and baptism: "In him also you were circumcised with a circumcision made without hands, by putting off the body of flesh in the circumcision of Christ; and you were buried with him in baptism" (Col. 2:11–12).

To some, this teaching seems to affirm that people without faith can be saved, so a few important points need to be made here to avoid confusion. First, the Church teaches that, as with circumcision, the grace of baptism can be lost. Just as an unfaithful person could be removed from the people of God after circumcision (e.g., Exod. 30:33, 38; Lev. 7:27; Num. 9:13; Prov. 2:22), an unfaithful Christian can fall from grace after baptism (Heb. 10:26–30; cf. Eph. 4:5). Thus, for anyone who can be *reasonably expected to have faith*, faith is required for salvation.

Many Protestants recognize this important qualification. Even those who strictly require faith for salvation will often admit that salvation remains possible for infants, those suffering severe mental disorder, or even those who simply never heard the gospel. Once again, there is an entire book devoted to various positions on this issue. In it, Protestant scholars debate between the *restrictivist* view (that knowledge of Jesus Christ in this life is necessary for salvation), the *divine perseverance* view (that those who die unevangelized are given an opportunity after death) and the *inclusivist* view (that some may be saved even if they do not know about Christ).[108]

IN PRINCIPLE

PROTESTANTS AGREE: God does save some people who cannot exercise personal faith through no fault of their own.

IN PARTICULAR

CATHOLICISM AFFIRMS: Through the faith of others, God saves those who cannot exercise personal faith.

We've seen that in discussions of salvation between Catholics and Protestants, a lot of headway toward accord can be made by clarifying terminology and considering foundational theological principles. When we take the time to do so, we may find that there is a lot more overlap than many recognize.[109] There is, however, one issue in Catholic theology that may not seem to have any analogue to Protestant belief whatsoever. That is the doctrine of purgatory.

Purgatory for Protestants?

Although it only takes up a couple sentences in the *Catechism*, the doctrine of purgatory seems to pose big problems for many Protestants.[110] As we will see, some of these problems result from misunderstandings—and once they are cleared up, what remains is not nearly as problematic as many Protestants imagine.

According to Catholic doctrine, purgatory is a place or a condition in which those who have died in a state of grace, but still have some minor sinful attachments, suffer temporal punishment in order to be fully purified for heaven. Believe it or not, that's pretty much it! Although there has been plenty of theological speculation, the Church has not defined purgatory in much more detail than that. Since every soul in purgatory is on its way to heaven, it's not a "third option" in the afterlife, as some may charge. Heaven and hell are the only final locations available to human beings. So purgatory is a temporary state of being for impure souls entering heaven. It will cease to exist after the resurrection (and perhaps before). There will be no need for purgatory once all heaven-bound souls arrive.

And although we casually speak of it in spatial and temporal terms, purgatory may not be a place at all, or even in time. Unfortunately, it is difficult and cumbersome to speak of disembodied souls in metaphysically accurate terms. It is much easier to say souls are *in* purgatory *for* X amount of time, just as it is easier to say God has been "in heaven since the beginning of time." Thus, it is important to keep in mind that these terms are being used in analogical or equivocal ways, and any criticisms based on seeing purgatory as a place in time are misplaced.

Even if the idea of purgatory as a "place" isn't considered a big deal by itself, it can lead to a related issue. Some Protestants reject purgatory because they think it contradicts Scripture. One proof for this contradiction popular with Evangelicals is the alleged scriptural principle that "to be absent from the body is to be present with the Lord." This is based on passages such as 2 Corinthians 5:6–8 and Philippians 1:23.[111] The idea is that because there is no intermediate step between death and heaven for those who are saved, there cannot be a purgatory in between. However, there is no verse in Scripture that actually says that "to be absent from the body is to be present with the Lord."[112]

Like "money is the root of all evil," or "all things work together for good," or "pride goes before a fall," or "the lion shall lie down with the lamb," the expression "to be absent from the body is to be present with the Lord" is simply a misquotation of Scripture. It is usually said to be 2 Corinthians 5:8 ("We are confident, I say, and willing rather to be absent from the body, and to be present with the Lord"— KJV) with occasional support coming from Philippians 1:23–24 ("My desire is to depart and be with Christ, for that is far better. But to remain in the flesh is more necessary on your account"). As is clear from the texts, however, Paul is expressing his *desire* to be absent from the body and present with the Lord—but desiring heaven does not guarantee its attainment (e.g., Paul's desire in Romans 9:3, or even God's desire in 2 Peter 3:9). Further, even if we take it on faith that Paul certainly made it to heaven after he died, his desire in no way implies that it would be immediate. When I lived in North Carolina my desire was to be at home with my family in California. Eventually that desire was satisfied, but I had to go many other places first!

Similarly, although the Church teaches that there are only two final "destinations" for people—heaven or hell—this does not preclude a temporary intermediate state. Many Protestants affirm that this at least was the case prior to Jesus' death and resurrection.[113] The traditional belief in a realm or state of the dead (variously referred to as *Sheol, Hades, Abraham's Bosom* or *Paradise*) that existed apart from one's final destination is biblically supported.[114] Thus, the idea of an afterlife state in addition to/apart from a *final* state (i.e., heaven or hell) is not unbiblical.

IN PRINCIPLE

PROTESTANTS AGREE: The fact that heaven and hell are the only two final destinations for all people that does not mean there cannot be an intermediate state for some.

IN PARTICULAR

CATHOLICISM AFFIRMS: Heaven and hell are the only two final destinations for all people, but for some there is an intermediate state.

Suppose I desired to be "absent from my office and present in my home." Although being absent from my office may be a necessary precondition for my being present in my home, it does not *guarantee* that I will be in my home or that I will be there *immediately* upon leaving my office; I could be picking up milk at the store on the way home from my office, for example. Finally, even if Paul had been expressing a certainty that *he* would be in the presence of the Lord the instant that he was not in his body, that would not mean that all people should have the same confidence (e.g., 2 Tim. 4:8; cf. James 1:12).[115] Indeed, as most Protestants agree, at least some who are absent from the body will end up in hell.

Catholics and Protestants can agree that we must understand Scripture for what it says and not add or subtract from it in order to support a principle it doesn't actually teach. Since neither 2 Corinthians 5:8 nor Philippians 1:23–24 is expressing a principle that strictly limits possible afterlife states, the passages do not prove anything for or against purgatory.

Sometimes Protestants object to purgatory as an answer to a question they didn't ask—namely, "How is a sinful person purified before entering the presence of God?" But since this *purification* aspect of salvation is not often emphasized in Protestant theology, they proceed to critique purgatory as if it were an answer to the question, "How does a sinful person escape hell?" This leads them to think purgatory is just another example of Catholic "works-salvation."

But this is not the case. Purgatory is not a second chance at salvation. All souls in purgatory are already saved and on their way to heaven. But even for one who is "saved"—in whom Christ's atonement has taken effect, sparing him damnation and putting him on the path to eternal life—sin has caused impurity of the soul. And this will simply not do in heaven, where nothing impure can enter (Rev. 21:27). Purgatory has been pictured as a sort of "antechamber" to heaven,[116] where the soul is purified to make it fit to be in God's presence.

Interestingly, most Protestants do not deny that this purification must take place. In his critique of the doctrine of purgatory, Evangelical scholar Ron Rhodes admits that "only perfectly righteous people get into heaven."[117] What they deny is that this necessary purification takes place between this life and heaven. For example, although claiming that "purgatory is a denial of the sufficiency of the cross," Evangelical apologist Norman Geisler does not argue against the need for purification from sins prior to heaven—he simply makes it part of the last step in the salvation process.[118]

Purgatory is suffering accompanied by joy, in which souls are "aflame" with the pain of desire for purification (see Romans 5:3-4) so they can survive the beatific vision of God (cf. Rev. 21:23-27). God's purification method is like that used for gold, which requires fiery heat to render it free of impurities (see Mal. 3:2–4; Dan. 11:35; Ps. 66:10–12; 1 Pet. 1:7). As a popular song in Evangelical circles goes:

Refiner's fire
My heart's one desire is to be holy . . .
Purify my heart, cleanse me from within and make me holy
Purify my heart, cleanse me from my sin, deep within.

Some Protestants say that this purifying fire is the suffering that believers experience in this life[119]—so it's not a huge stretch to believe that final purification also can be accomplished through suffering undergone after death. Even for Protestants who grasp the connection between suffering and sanctification, purgatory can sound like a place where people are expected to pay for their sins. Didn't Jesus already pay for them on the cross?

The Church teaches that Jesus paid for the *eternal* consequences of sin (damnation in hell), but that sin also carries
with it *temporal* consequences: repercussions to atone for, personal imperfections and attachments that must be worked out
in this life or the next. As the classic analogy goes: If a child
disobeys his father and plays baseball inside the house, caus-
ing a broken window, the father may forgive the son of his
disobedience—but the son must still pay to fix the window.

We see a template for this distinction in Scripture. For
example, God forgave Adam and Eve—but they still suffered the consequences of the fall. God forgave Moses but
did not let him enter the Promised Land. These biblical
figures weren't damned for their sins, and they were later
saved by Christ's blood, but they had to undergo suffering
for their sins, too.

And we recognize this in our own lives, where the consequences of sin—on our relationships, on our habits, on our
desires—remain and must be repaired even when we are in
a state of grace. It's best to repair these things and become
purified in this life by voluntary sacrifice, suffering, and
repentance (Matt. 3:8; Luke 3:3, 17:3; Rom. 5:3–5; Heb.
12:11–14), but if we don't accomplish it all before death, purgatory allows us to experience purification by doing pen-
ance for those sins left temporally "unpaid."

IN PRINCIPLE

PROTESTANTS AGREE: Suffering in this life can
purify us and prepare us for the reward of heaven.

IN PARTICULAR

CATHOLICISM AFFIRMS: Suffering in the afterlife
purifies and prepares us for the reward of heaven.

Even if accord with Protestants can be reached on some of the theological principles supporting purgatory, the question may arise, "But where is it in the Bible?"

Catholics, of course, can turn to 2 Maccabees 12:45, which speaks of prayers of atonement being offered on behalf of the dead to deliver them from their sins. But this book is one of the seven that Protestants removed from the canon of Scripture, considering them non-inspired "apocrypha."[120] (Though it could be argued that, even if not inspired, it's indicative of Jewish thought in the time shortly before the birth of Christ.) But we can also find support for purgatory in a biblical book that Protestants do accept. In 1 Corinthians 3:11–15, we see *saved* people being judged and suffering loss based on what they did in this life:

For no other foundation can anyone lay than that which is laid, which is Jesus Christ. Now if any one builds on the foundation with gold, silver, precious stones, wood, hay, stubble—each man's work will become manifest; for the Day will disclose it, because it will be revealed with fire, and the fire will test what sort of work each one has done. If the work which any man has built on the foundation survives, he will receive a reward. If any man's work is burned up, he will suffer loss, though he himself will be saved, but only as through fire.

Of course, individual readers may interpret verses like this differently. But that's the case with verses often cited to support many other Christian beliefs, too. Foundational doctrines such as the Trinity and the Incarnation have no texts that simply spell the doctrines out, and there exist some seriously difficult counter-prooftexts to deal with (ask any Jehovah's Witness!). These dogmas took centuries to clarify to the level they exist at today. Protestants did not simply open their Bibles and discover them, so they should not expect to do so with purgatory. And so we return to the need for Sacred Tradition to inform and for an authoritative Church to interpret Scripture in the way that will unite all Christians in truth.

IN PRINCIPLE

PROTESTANTS AGREE: Christians have impure works judged by God resulting in reward or punishment.

IN PARTICULAR

CATHOLICISM AFFIRMS: Christians have impure works judged by God resulting in reward or punishment in purgatory.

Indulge Me for a Minute

It's fitting to end not just this section on purgatory but our book on accord between Catholics and Protestants with the primary issue that launched the Reformation. Although issues such as justification by faith alone, religious reliance on Scripture alone, Marian beliefs, and sacraments might seem to be the major difficulties that the two groups face today, this was not the case when Martin Luther posted his Ninety-Five Theses in 1517.

It may come as a surprise to many modern Protestants, but Luther did not (initially) challenge the necessity of good works or the existence of purgatory. In fact, his Theses *presume* them. Luther's main objection, instead, revolved around the selling of indulgences—and rightly so. This corrupt practice would soon be addressed and outlawed at the Council of Trent.

Indulgences do not take up a lot of space in Catholic theology. The *Catechism*, for example, devotes only eight of its 2,865 sections to discussing them. But they have great symbolic value as a poster-issue for Protestant criticism of the Church.

Some Protestants mistakenly believe indulgences to be a permission to "indulge" in sin—a legalistic free pass that keeps you from hell no matter what you do. But indulgences do not (and have never) gotten anyone out of hell or into heaven. As "a remission before God of the temporal punishment due to sins whose guilt has already been forgiven" (*Indulgentarium Doctrina* 1), they are useful only for those who die in a state of grace and are on their way to heaven.

As we noted above, before we can enter heaven we must repair or atone for the temporal punishment due to sin, either through penitential acts of prayer and suffering voluntarily chosen on earth or suffering involuntarily endured after death. But the Church provides another way of satisfying the debt of temporal punishment, which it is able to extend to the faithful by virtue of the power, given to it by Jesus, to bind and loose (Matt. 16:19, 18:17–19) and to forgive sins (John 20:23). In granting indulgences, the Church formally endows certain prayers and pious acts with a penitential character. Some of those prayer or acts, when performed under certain prescribed circumstances, effect full or *plenary* indulgences, able to remit the entirety of one's temporal punishment due to sin.

Indulgences can be gained in a number of ways so long as one is properly disposed to receive them. Indulgenced acts include spending time in devout prayer, reading Sacred Scripture, and going on pilgrimages to sacred sites. They may be attached to certain holy days, or to special events in the life of the Church or of individual believers.

Protestants agree that doing such things are spiritually beneficial. What Protestant has not been told that Scripture study or prayer is important (if not essential!) to a fully Christian spiritual life? So it is not that Protestants deny their spiritual value; they simply don't give them the formal status as tools of sanctification that Catholic theology does. This, however, seems to be more of a difference than a distinction.

Of course, Catholics apply this spiritual principle to the Church's other teachings regarding salvation. Thus, although the culture of indulgences might seem foreign to Protestants, in truth it's not much more than a way to quantify and officially recognize practices that they already agree provide spiritual benefit.

IN PRINCIPLE

PROTESTANTS AGREE: Faithful actions such as prayer and Scripture reading are spiritually beneficial.

IN PARTICULAR

CATHOLICISM AFFIRMS: Faithful actions such as prayer and Scripture reading are spiritually beneficial as penances for the temporal results of sin.

Catholics and Protestants can agree on the need to atone for sin, the lasting temporal effects of sins even after they're forgiven, and the absolute incompatibility of heaven with any kind of spiritual flaw. The Catholic doctrine of purgatory does not pose a third eternal state; it does not contradict Jesus' sufficiency for salvation; and it is neither legalistic or unbiblical. Whether it involves literal purifying fire, climbing a great mountain, or some state completely divorced from both time and space, *something* happens to cause this purification.

Anyone, including Protestants, who believes that people who are impure in this life are pure in the afterlife believes in a kind of purgatory even if he doesn't call it that. Building on these points, it may be possible to reach a great deal of accord even on this classic dividing line between us.

Of all the potential areas for division between Catholics and Protestants, nothing is more important than beliefs surrounding salvation. With literally hundreds of potential areas of disagreement between (and, often, within!) these two groups, accord simply cannot be fully realized apart from agreement on the foundational issue of attaining eternal life.

A famous dictum states that Christians must have unity in essentials, liberty in non-essentials, and charity in all things. Although this saying's pedigree is questionable, there is some truth to it.[121] As Norman Geisler and Ron Rhodes state it, "Judging by the doctrines pronounced essential by the historic Christian church, an essential doctrine is one connected with our salvation."[122] At the end of the day, our various disagreements will not amount to much so long as we enter God's glory together.

Although neither Catholics nor Protestants may compromise our soteriological commitments, we can pursue greater accord by taking the necessary time (likely quite a bit of it) to truly and deeply understand each other's positions. And this cannot be merely a superficial ability to spit back each other's particular salvation statements—we must go deep into the foundational principles that give rise to them.

Unity and Division

It is to be numbered among the evils of our day, that the churches are so divided one from another, that there is scarcely any friendly intercourse strengthened between us; much less does that holy communion of the members of Christ flourish, which all profess with the mouth, but few sincerely regard in the heart. . . . Thus it comes to pass, that the members being divided, the body of the church lies disabled. Respecting myself, if it should appear that I could render any service, I should with pleasure cross ten seas, if necessary, to accomplish that object.

—John Calvin[123]

In St. John's Gospel, Jesus prayed for Christian unity—specifically "that they may all be one; even as thou, Father, art in me, and I in thee, that they also may be in us, so that the world may believe that thou hast sent me" (John 17:21). There is a connection between Christian unity and the belief of others. When Christians, "who believe in me through their [the apostles'] word" are unified, the world sees something worth believing. It is clear both in theory and in practice that the opposite is also true. In a divided Christendom, the world may see something that can't be trusted.

St. Paul pleaded that this principle be put into action. "I appeal to you, brethren, by the name of our Lord Jesus Christ, that all of you agree and that there be no dissensions among you, but that you be united in the same mind and the same judgment" (1 Cor. 1:10). He begged believers to "maintain the unity of the Spirit in the bond of peace" (Eph. 4:3). St. Peter, too, asserted to "all of you [Christians], have unity of spirit, sympathy, love of the brethren, a tender heart and a humble mind" (1 Pet. 3:8). If unity and love go together (e.g., Col. 3:14; Phil. 2:2), and display faithfulness to God as we have seen (see also John 15:12–19), then disunity indicates the opposite. How can Christians be witnesses of the truth of Christ when all the world sees are divisions?

When it comes to Protestant disagreement with Catholics, one step is to recognize that the issues are very often not at the level of consistently held principles, but at that of *inconsistent particulars*. What we have seen throughout this book is a continued pattern of principles inconsistently applied.

Numerous examples have been given in this book that show that the real problem often lies outside Protestant principles. When we're able to look more closely at Catholic teachings that Protestants reject, when we look at the *why* behind the *what*, we can see that many of them are in accord with sound principles that Protestants generally hold even if they haven't acknowledged or fully explored them.

If both sides see that they often agree in principle far more than they disagree over particulars, greater headway can be made toward restoration of the unity that Jesus Christ prayed for and St. Paul commanded. We may yet discover a way back to the accord that the Church experienced fifteen centuries before the theological discord of the last five centuries began. And if we can do so, we may also recover the witness of the early Church that resulted in the conversion of the world (Rom. 1:8).

ENDNOTES

1   See Philippians 3:5.

2   As it turned out, I wasn't alone. Numerous professors and alumni from my seminary eventually became Catholic. Many of our stories and arguments are detailed in the book *Evangelical Exodus* (Ignatius, 2016).

3   The word *canon* is a Greek term that originally meant a straight rod or rule—a criterion. It began to be applied by Christian writers of the later fourth century to the correct collection and list of the scriptures.

4   As Evangelical scholar Craig Allert put it, "Surely what the Bible is has much importance for what the Bible says." (Craig Allert, *A High View of Scripture?*, 11).

5   Athanasius's Festal Letter 39 (A.D. 367) was the first place that the term *canon* was used to specify the content of the New Testament, and it is the first to match the finalized twenty-seven-book list. The first list to exactly match the Catholic canon was produced by the Council of Rome in A.D. 382. This canon was later ratified by the Councils of Hippo (393) and Carthage (397). Pope Innocent I put forth the same list in 405, and the next council of Carthage (419) approved it as well. These were local rulings, however, and were not considered binding on the entire Church.

6   See Yves Congar, *The Meaning of Tradition*, ch. 3.

7   Norman Geisler and Ralph MacKenzie, *Roman Catholics and Evangelicals: Agreements and Differences* (Baker, 1995), 192–193. It is interesting to note that some of the criteria that is used to merely "discover" the inspired books (e.g., authorship or acceptance) are themselves reliant on Church Tradition.

8   See Denzinger, *Sources of Catholic Dogma*, 1787.

9   For the vast majority of Protestants, this remains true. Despite Martin Luther's rejection of seven Old Testament books and his attack on some New Testament books, no Protestant denomination has tampered with the New Testament canon that Rome settled in the fourth century.

10 "Evangelicals and the Canon," 29.

11 St. Vincent of Lerins noted that "if one should ask one of the heretics, . . . 'What ground have you, for saying, that I ought to cast away the universal and ancient faith of the Catholic Church?' He has the answer ready: 'For it is written,' and forthwith he produces a thousand testimonies, a thousand examples, a thousand authorities from the Law, from the Psalms, from the apostles, from the Prophets, by means of which, interpreted on a new and wrong principle, the unhappy soul may be precipitated from the height of Catholic truth to the lowest abyss of heresy. . . . Do heretics also appeal to Scripture? They do indeed, and with a vengeance . . . hardly ever do they bring forward anything of their own which they do not endeavor to shelter under words of Scripture. . . . an infinite heap of instances, hardly a single page, which does not bristle with plausible quotations from the New Testament or the Old" (Commonitory, 25–A.D. 434).

12 Some people make a mistake and argue that if the Church is necessary to interpret the Bible then we must also need some kind of interpretive authority to understand the Church. But it is not as though the Catholic point rests on some kind of linguistic skepticism where every communication requires an additional interpreter. The difference between two contemporary people coming from similar backgrounds com-

municating in the same language and understanding a collection of books written in dead languages, from foreign cultures, by dozens of different authors from different backgrounds and cultures is so great that the two really should not even be compared.

13 Thomas Aquinas, *Summa Theologiae* II.2.11.

14 For example, popular Protestant blogger Matt Slick writes, "To me, it is not enough to simply say that Sacred Tradition is equal to Scripture based upon the decree of the Catholic Magisterium. Like any spiritual teaching, I must compare it to the Bible. . . . If Scripture is 'within the living Tradition,' then Tradition encompasses Scripture. In other words, it is the tradition of the Church that interprets Scripture. This is in contradiction to the Word of God spoken by Jesus in Matt. 15:1–6." (*Roman Catholicism, the Bible, and Tradition* found at carm.org/catholic/roman-catholicism-bible-and-tradition on 05.15.19) Note that Matthew 15:1–6 says nothing of the sort. In this passage, Jesus accuses the religious leaders of contradicting God's Word with their man-made tradition. The problem is the contradiction, not the tradition (cf. 2 Thess. 2:15 and 3:6).

15 See James R. Payton Jr., *Getting the Reformation Wrong: Correcting Some Misunderstandings* (Downers Grove, IL, IVP Academic, 2010), 132–159.

16 Luther's view was historically unprecedented. As Protestant scholar Alister McGrath concluded in his monumental study, although the Reformation's understanding of the mode of justification was not a new teaching, "The Protestant understanding of the nature of justification represents a theological novum." Alister McGrath, *Iustitia Dei: A History of the Christian Doctrine of Justification* (3rd ed.) (Cambridge: 2005), 184.

17 *Luther's Works* (Fortress Press, 1958, volume 32, page 112). Note that these words are disputed by some scholars.

18 This is especially the case in the New Testament which was written in a sort of street-level version of the Greek language (Koine) that would not have impressed anyone in the first century! What makes supernatural revelation special is not the words but their source.

19 This is the distinction between *material* and *formal* sufficiency. Having the ingredients (*matter*) for pancakes, waffles, or biscuits, is not sufficient to limit these ingredients to only one dish. That requires a recipe (*form*). Material without form can be made into too many things (even though it cannot be made into absolutely anything). This is true of interpretations as well as ingredients.

20 One book presents five contrary views on the nature of "justification" (James K. Beilby and Paul Rhodes Eddy, *Justification: Five Views*. IVP Academic, 2011). What qualifies as "faith" launched an ongoing theological war between two major camps known as "Free Grace" and "Lordship Salvation" (e.g. John MacArthur and Zane Hodges longstanding feud). Finally, how exactly good works relate to faith (i.e., how faith is "alone") in Protestantism runs the spectrum from legalism to licentiousness.

21 By the end of the twentieth century, the Catholic Church had held twenty-one such councils. They are called *ecumenical* (from the Greek *oikoumene,* referring to the known inhabited world) because their declarations are authoritatively and universally binding on the faithful.

22 The force of this example might be lessened by the claim that God simply revealed these things directly to the biblical writers. However, this seems to assume a dictation view of inspiration, which most scholars—both Catholic and Protestant—reject.

23 E.g., Norman Geisler and Ralph MacKenzie, *Roman Catholics and Evangelicals: Agreements and Differences* (Baker, 1995), 157.

24 In fact, there are some fringe Protestant groups that argue against such things on this basis.

25 This is apparently why Martin Luther added the word *alone* to his German translation of Romans 3:28.

26 See "Marcionites" in the *Catholic Encyclopedia*, at https://www.newadvent.org/cathen/09645c.htm.

27 Jehovah's Witnesses, headed by the Watchtower organization, deny the divinity of Jesus Christ. However, they are not considered a legitimate Christian group by the Catholic Church or any Protestant denomination.

28 The Watchtower Society's *New World Translation* is an especially egregious example of theologically biased mistranslation that is used to support the heretical theology of the Jehovah's Witnesses. See https://douglasbeaumont.com/?s=watchtower.

29 Protestant historical theologian Alister McGrath concluded his study of the doctrine of justification by saying a "fundamental discontinuity was introduced into the western theological tradition where none had ever existed, or ever been contemplated, before. The Reformation understanding of the nature of justification as opposed to its mode must therefore be regarded as a genuine theological *novum*" (Alister McGrath, *Iustitia Dei: A History of the Christian Doctrine of Justification*, 186).

30 An example of theological bias seems to be reflected in the New International Version—the most popular modern translation of the Bible among Evangelical Protestants. Throughout the text, the Greek word *paradosis* is correctly translated as "tradition" (e.g., Matt. 15:1–5; Gal. 1:14; Col. 2:8); however, in a handful of verses it is translated as "teaching" (e.g., 1 Cor. 11:2; 2 Thess. 2:14, 3:6). Upon inspection, it seems clear that the translators made this decision in order to support the Protestant view of tradition. That is, whenever *paradosis* is spoken of negatively it is translated as "tradition,' but when it is spoken of positively, it is translated as "teaching."

31 Norman L. Geisler and Ralph E. MacKenzie, *Roman Catholics and Evangelicals: Agreements and Differences* (Grand Rapids, MI: Baker Books, 1995), 167.

32 The assertion that the author of 1 Maccabees claims not to be a prophet is a stretch at best. Nowhere does the author make a self-referential statement to this effect. What he says is simply that "there was great distress in Israel, such as had not been since the time that prophets ceased to appear among them." The author is reporting a past event that began when prophetic activity ceased for a while. Such time periods are not unusual. Even in the Bible, prophetic writings are not continuous states—rather, they stand out precisely because they are unusual (e.g., Moses, Elijah, Jesus, the apostles). That the author of 1 Maccabees is reporting on one such time period is no indication that prophets would never come on the scene again (cf. 1 Maccabees 14:41). Finally, there is no statement anywhere in the Bible that prophecy ceased during the so-called "Intertestamental Period"—it may even indicate the opposite (e.g., the prophets listed in Luke 1–2, cf. Matt. 11:13). For more on this subject, see Joe Heschmeyer, "Was Christ's Birth Preceded by 400 Years of Divine Silence?" (shamelesspopery.com/was-christs-birth-preceded-by-400-years-of-divine-silence/).

33 *Luther's Works*, vol. 54: Table Talk.

34 For an impressive collection of just such texts, see Karlo Broussard's *Meeting the Protestant Challenge* (Catholic Answers, 2019) or Patrick Madrid's *Where Is That in the Bible?* (Our Sunday Visitor, 2001).

35 The popular Protestant website *Got Questions?* puts it this way: "Most religion, theistic or otherwise, is man-centered. Any relationship with God is based on man's works." (https://www.gotquestions.org/Christianity-religion-relationship.html). A more academic treatment says, "One of the reasons so many Roman Catholic lay persons are converting to evangelicalism is that they did not find a dynamic personal relationship

with Christ in their Catholic church. The reality is often lost in the ritual." Norman L. Geisler and Ralph E. MacKenzie, *Roman Catholics and Evangelicals: Agreements and Differences* (Grand Rapids, MI: Baker Books, 1995), 392.

36 A movement known as the "New Perspective on Paul" has arisen in Protestant scholarship, headed by notable theologians such as E.P. Sanders, N.T. Wright, and James Dunn. The central claim is that the idea of Jewish religious "legalism" is a product of Martin Luther and other Reformers' misunderstanding of St. Paul.

37 "βατταλογέω" in William Arndt, F. Wilbur Gingrich, Frederick W. Danker, et al., *A Greek-English Lexicon of the New Testament and Other Early Christian Literature* (Chicago: University of Chicago Press, 1979), 137.

38 Perhaps this was allowed to happen because God wanted to show Saul how far he had fallen. It was Saul's job to rid the land of mediums (1 Sam. 28:3), and yet now—because he had not listened to God through Samuel before (1 Sam. 28:17–18)—he required a medium to hear from God through Samuel.

39 For example, *proseuchomai* in Matthew 6 compared to *deomai* in Luke 8:28 or *euchomai* in Romans 9:3. See *A Greek-English Lexicon Of The New Testament and Other Early Christian Literature*, William Arndt, F. Wilbur Gingrich, Frederick W. Danker, et al. (Chicago: University of Chicago Press, 1979).

40 "It is an undeniable fact that devotion to Mary among Catholics far exceeds devotion to God or Christ." Dave Hunt, *A Woman Rides the Beast* (Eugene, OR: Harvest House, 1994), 444.

41 "The theoretical distinctions notwithstanding, on the experiential level, there appears to be little if any difference between the intensity of this devotion to Mary and the worship of God." Norman L. Geisler and Ralph E. MacKenzie, *Roman Catholics and Evangelicals: Agreements and Differences* (Grand Rapids, MI: Baker Books, 1995), 323.

42 "Though the Catholic Church claims it does not worship Mary, it comes as close as is possible to doing just that. . . . The Church says God is due *cultus latriae* (adoration), the angels are due *cultus duliae* (veneration), but Mary may receive *hyperduliae* [*sic*] (or special veneration)! However, in A.D. 373, St. Ephrem wrote hymns which "are almost equally songs of praise for the Virgin Mother" as those written about the Lord! The Church admits that Mary was glorified in numerous sermons and hymns in her honor during the Middle Ages. Many festivals and feast days are held in her honor, such as the Feast of her Home-Going (Assumption), and her birth." Mal Couch, "The Heretical Teaching of Catholic Mariology," *Conservative Theological Journal Volume 5*, no. 15 (2001): 161–162.

43 "*Proskuneo*" in James Strong, *Enhanced Strong's Lexicon* (Woodside Bible Fellowship, 1995).

44 "*Proskuneo*" in William Arndt et al., *A Greek-English Lexicon of the New Testament and Other Early Christian Literature* (Chicago: University of Chicago Press, 1979), 716–717.

45 *Summa Theologiae* II–II. Q.103 A.4 and III. Q.25 A.5.

46 These three kinds of objects are known as *first*, *second*, and *third* class relics respectively.

47 Some use the term "ordinance" to distinguish them from proper sacraments.

48 This follows from *sola fide* ("faith alone") salvation theory, although actions are often expected to occur later if the mental conversion was real.

49 The famous Evangelical salvation tracts "The Romans Road" and "The Four Spiritual Laws" are prime examples of this viewpoint.

50 Protestants sometimes will say that humans *are* souls but *have* bodies.

51 The Church teaches that God's saving grace comes *ordinarily* through the sacraments but is not bound by them. Luke 23:33–43 cf. CCC 1257–1261.

52 Sacraments confer grace *ex opere operato*, "by the work worked," not *ex opere operantis*, "by the work of the worker."

53   Norman L. Geisler and Ralph E. MacKenzie, *Roman Catholics and Evangelicals: Agreements and Differences* (Grand Rapids, MI: Baker Books, 1995), 264.

54   Dave Hunt, *A Woman Rides the Beast* (Eugene, OR: Harvest House, 1994), 383.

55   Norman L. Geisler and Ralph E. MacKenzie, *Roman Catholics and Evangelicals: Agreements and Differences* (Grand Rapids, MI: Baker Books, 1995), 265.

56   One Bengarius of Tours was said to be the first to seriously dispute this teaching, in the eleventh century. He eventually recanted.

57   Even Ulrich Zwingli, one of the most radically non-Catholic of the Reformers, stated, "It seems to me the dear saints and the Virgin Mary are not to be despised, since there are few who have not felt the intercession of the Virgin and the saints. I do not care what everyone says or believes. I have placed a ladder against heaven; I believe firmly in the intercession of the much-praised queen of heaven, the mother of God, and another may believe or hold what he pleases" (*Selected Works of Huldreich Zwingli, (1484–1531): The Reformer of German Switzerland*. Samuel Macauley Jackson, ed. (Philadelphia, PA: University of Pennsylvania, 1901), 84.

58   Norman L. Geisler and Ron Rhodes, *When Cultists Ask: A Popular Handbook on Cultic Misinterpretations* (Grand Rapids, MI: Baker Books, 1997), 96.

59   Donald Guthrie, *New Testament Introduction*, 4th rev. ed., The Master Reference Collection (Downers Grove, IL: InterVarsity Press, 1996), 801.

60   W.E. Vine, *Collected Writings of W.E. Vine* (Nashville, TN: Thomas Nelson, 1996), 1 Thessalonians 5:11.

61   Luther, *On the Councils and Churches*, 1539, WLS I, p. 198 in Thomas C. Oden, *The Word of Life: Systematic Theology*, Vol. II (San Francisco, CA: HarperSanFrancisco, 1992), 341.

62   Again, with Luther, Christians affirm, "Since Christ is the Son both of God and of Mary in one indivisible Person with two distinct natures, we correctly say of the entire Person: God is crucified for us, God shed His blood for us; God died for us and rose from the dead," [Luther, *Sermon on Col. 1:18–20*, WLS I, p. 193 in Thomas C. Oden, *The Word of Life: Systematic Theology*, Vol. II (San Francisco, CA: HarperSanFrancisco, 1992), 341].

63   Evangelical apologist Eric Svendsen makes a rather stunning theological gaffe in his arguments against Mary's title. He asserts that "if we are to accept this argument, then we must also accept its logical extension: Major Premise: God is Trinity. Minor Premise: Mary is the mother of God. Conclusion: Mary is the mother of the Trinity." *Evangelical Answers: A Critique of Current Roman Catholic Apologists* (Lindenhurst, NY: Reformation Press, 1999), 128. This argument is of the same kind that Jehovah's Witnesses and other Arians make against Jesus being God incarnate and only seems to make sense as part of a denial of the orthodox view of the Trinity. If God is one *essence* but three *persons,* and Jesus is only one of those persons, then Mary's motherhood would not extend to the entirety of the Godhead. Perhaps even more incredible is Reformed apologist James White's endorsement of the book, given that White himself has authored a defense of the Trinity!

64   Evangelical scholar Norman Geisler emphasizes this point: "Mary conceived 'before they came together,' thus revealing that it was not a natural conception. Second, Joseph's initial reaction reveals that he had not had sexual intercourse with Mary, since when he found that she was pregnant 'he had in mind to divorce her quietly.' Third, the phrase 'what is conceived in her is from the Holy Spirit' reveals the supernatural nature of the event. Finally, the citation from the Septuagint translation of Isaiah 7:14

about a *parthenos*, 'virgin,' giving 'birth' to a child indicates that Mary had not had sexual relations with anyone. She was not simply a virgin before the baby was conceived, but after it was conceived and even when it was born." Norman L. Geisler, "Virgin Birth of Christ," *Baker Encyclopedia of Christian Apologetics*, Baker Reference Library (Grand Rapids, MI: Baker Books, 1999), 762.

65   Greek, "*Epei ginosko ou andra.*"

66   I owe this insight to the anonymous creator of the "How To Be Christian" YouTube channel (see https://youtu.be/PKTsWVKPAwY).

67   Grant Osborne (Professor of New Testament at Trinity Evangelical Divinity School) devotes the entire first chapter of his famed treatise on biblical hermeneutics to issues of context in interpretation. See Grant R. Osborne, *The Hermeneutical Spiral: A Comprehensive Introduction to Biblical Interpretation* (Downers Grove, IL: InterVarsity Press, 1991). Reformed Evangelical scholar D.A. Carson, in his popular book devoted to mistakes in biblical interpretation, says, "We sometimes fail to appreciate how wide the total semantic range of a word is; therefore when we come to perform the exegesis of a particular passage, we do not adequately consider the potential options and unwittingly exclude possibilities that might include the correct one." [D.A. Carson, *Exegetical Fallacies*, 2nd ed. (Carlisle, U.K.; Grand Rapids, MI: Paternoster; Baker Books, 1996), 28, 57.] In his response to the Catholic view of this very passage, Norman Geisler admits, "It is true that the words for brother and sister can mean close relative. This must be determined by the context and from other scriptures." Norman L. Geisler and Thomas A. Howe, *When Critics Ask: A Popular Handbook on Bible Difficulties* (Wheaton, IL: Victor Books, 1992), 346.

68   "I am inclined to agree with those who declare that 'brothers' really means 'cousins' here, for Holy Writ and the Jews always call cousins brothers." Martin Luther, *Luther's Works, Vol. 22: Sermons on the Gospel of St. John: Chapters 1–4*, ed. Jaroslav Jan Pelikan, Hilton C. Oswald, and Helmut T. Lehmann, vol. 22 (Saint Louis: Concordia Publishing House, 1999), 214–215.

69   "The word brothers, we have formerly mentioned, is employed, agreeably to the Hebrew idiom, to denote any relatives whatever; and, accordingly, Helvidius displayed excessive ignorance in concluding that Mary must have had many sons, because Christ's brothers are sometimes mentioned." John Calvin and William Pringle, *Commentary on a Harmony of the Evangelists Matthew, Mark, and Luke*, vol. 2 (Bellingham, WA: Logos Bible Software, 2010), 215.

70   "I firmly believe that Mary, according to the words of the gospel as a pure Virgin brought forth for us the Son of God and in childbirth and after childbirth forever remained a pure, intact Virgin." Ulrich Zwingli, *Opera Corpus Reformatorum*, Berlin, Volume 1: 424.

71   William Arndt et al., *A Greek-English Lexicon of the New Testament and Other Early Christian Literature* (Chicago: University of Chicago Press, 1979), 334.

72   Example credit goes to "MDYK: Was Mary a Perpetual Virgin?" at YouTube.com.

73   "Now this refutes also the false interpretation which some have drawn from the words of Matthew, where he says, 'Before they came together she was found to be with child.' They interpret this as though the evangelist meant to say, "Later she came together with Joseph like any other wife and lay with him, but before this occurred she was with child apart from Joseph," etc. Again, when he says, 'And Joseph knew her not until she brought forth her first-born son,' they interpret it as though the evangelist meant to say that he knew her, but not before she had brought forth her first-born son. This was the view of Helvidius which was refuted by Jerome. Such carnal interpretations miss

the meaning and purpose of the evangelist. As we have said, the evangelist, like the prophet Isaiah, wishes to set before our eyes this mighty wonder, and point out what an unheard-of thing it is for a maiden to be with child before her husband brings her home and lies with her; and further, that he does not know her carnally until she first has a son, which she should have had after first having been known by him. Thus, the words of the evangelist do not refer to anything that occurred after the birth, but only to what took place before it." Martin Luther, *Luther's Works, Vol. 45 : The Christian in Society II*, ed. Jaroslav Jan Pelikan, Hilton C. Oswald, and Helmut T. Lehmann, vol. 45 (Philadelphia: Fortress Press, 1999), 211–212.

74   "This passage afforded the pretext for great disturbances, which were introduced into the Church, at a former period, by Helvidius. The inference he drew from it was, that Mary remained a virgin no longer than till her first birth, and that afterward she had other children by her husband. . . . no just and well-grounded inference can be drawn from these words of the Evangelist . . . What took place afterward, the historian does not inform us. Such is well known to have been the practice of the inspired writers. Certainly, no man will ever raise a question on this subject, except from curiosity; and no man will obstinately keep up the argument, except from an extreme fondness for disputation." John Calvin and William Pringle, *Commentary on a Harmony of the Evangelists Matthew, Mark, and Luke*, vol. 1 (Bellingham, WA: Logos Bible Software, 2010), 107.

75   Popular Evangelical apologists regularly rely on Church tradition for one of their arguments concerning the resurrection of Jesus: namely, that the martyrdom of the apostles proves they were not lying about the Resurrection. Top Resurrection scholar and apologist Gary Habermas includes the martyrdom of the apostles as one of the nearly uncontested facts of New Testament history [see Gary Habermas, *The Resurrection of Jesus* (Lanham, MD: University Press of America), 34]. Popular Evangelical speaker and teacher Sean McDowell says, "The willingness of the apostles to suffer and die for their faith is one of the most commonly cited arguments for the Resurrection. Yet what is the evidence they actually died as martyrs?" ("Did the Apostles Really Die as Martyrs for Their Faith?" available at www.equip.org/article/apostles-really-die-martyrs-faith). Evangelical apologist Frank Turek argues that "the New Testament writers suffered persecution and death when they could have saved themselves by recanting. If they had made up the Resurrection story, they certainly would have said so when they were about to be crucified (Peter), stoned (James), or beheaded (Paul). But no one recanted—eleven out of the twelve were martyred for their faith (the only survivor was John, who was exiled to the Greek island of Patmos). Why would they die for a known lie?" Norman L. Geisler and Frank Turek, *I Don't Have Enough Faith to Be an Atheist* (Wheaton, IL: Crossway Books, 2004), 292.

76   This confusion is reflected in the popular website *Got Questions?* (a website to which I used to contribute): https://www.gotquestions.org/Queen-of-Heaven.html.

77   Muslims have made this mistaken accusation based on the *Quran* sura 5:73, 116.

78   Theology by etymology is rarely a trustworthy practice. The Christian faith did not originate in a verbal vacuum, and the Church regularly conscripts ideas and terms to express the truth. (St. Paul, for example, quoted pagan poets to make points—e.g., Acts 17:28; 1 Corinthians 15:33; Titus 1:12.) One rather humorous example is the word we translate as *baptism*," which is a transliteration of a word found in a recipe for making pickles!

79   For a rigorous scientific evaluation of this phenomena, see Stanley Jaki's *God and the Sun at Fatima*.

80   Norman L. Geisler and Ralph E. MacKenzie, *Roman Catholics and Evangelicals: Agreements and Differences* (Grand Rapids, MI: Baker Books, 1995), 144.

81   For example, John Calvin claims that, "The apostle, however, does not here [1 John 5:16–17] distinguish between venial and mortal sin, as it was afterward commonly done. For altogether foolish is that distinction which prevails under the papacy." John Calvin *Commentaries on the Catholic Epistles.* Tr. John Owen (Bellingham, WA: Logos Bible Software, 2010), 268.

82   John Calvin writes, "But among the faithful this ought to be an indubitable truth, that whatever is contrary to God's law is sin, and in its nature mortal; for where there is a transgression of the law, there is sin and death. What, then, is the meaning of the Apostle? He denies that sins are mortal, which, though worthy of death, are yet not thus punished by God. He therefore does not estimate sins in themselves, but forms a judgment of them according to the paternal kindness of God, which pardons the guilt, where yet the fault is. In short, God does not give over to death those whom he has restored to life, though it depends not on them that they are not alienated from life. *There is a sin unto death.* I have already said that the sin to which there is no hope of pardon left, is thus called. But it may be asked, what this is; for it must be very atrocious, when God thus so severely punishes it. It may be gathered from the context, that it is not, as they say, a partial fall, or a transgression of a single commandment, but apostasy, by which men wholly alienate themselves from God." John Calvin *Commentaries on the Catholic Epistles.* Tr. John Owen (Bellingham, WA: Logos Bible Software, 2010), 269.

83   See the work of John MacArthur such as *The Gospel According to Jesus* (Grand Rapids, MI: Zondervan, 2008).

84   See the work of Zane Hodges such as *Absolutely Free: A Biblical Reply to Lordship Salvation* (Corinth, TX: Grace Evangelical Society, 2014).

85   Thomas Aquinas, *Summa Theologiae,* ST I–II, Q. 91, A. 2.

86   See Geisler's *Ethics: Alternatives and Issues* (Grand Rapids, MI: Zondervan, 1971), 218–227 and his *Christian Ethics: Options and Issues* (Grand Rapids, MI: Baker Book house, 1989), 135–154.

87   E.g., *Didache* 2:2.

88   James K. Beilby and Paul Rhodes Eddy, *Justification: Five Views* (Downers Grove, IL: InterVarsity, 2011).

89   Zondervan's *Counterpoints* series (zondervanacademic.com/products/category/counter-points) and InterVarsity's Spectrum (www.ivpress.com/spectrum-multiview-book-series) are good examples of these kinds of "multi-view" books.

90   For example, Arminians teach that salvation can be lost and "Free Grace" Protestants believe that good works increase our reward in heaven.

91   "'Our justification is not yet complete. . . . It is still under construction. It shall, however, be completed in the resurrection of the dead (WA 391, 252).' This sense of progressive justification is what many Protestants call 'sanctification,' the process by which we are *made* righteous, not an act by which one is *declared* righteous." Norman L. Geisler and Ralph E. MacKenzie, *Roman Catholics and Evangelicals: Agreements and Differences* (Grand Rapids, MI: Baker Books, 1995), 222–223.

92   Alister E. McGrath, *Iustitia Dei: A History of the Christian Doctrine of Justification, The Beginnings to the Reformation* (New York, NY: Cambridge University Press, 1997), 182.

93   Ibid.

94   Council of Trent, "On Justification," VIII.

95   Guy Prentiss Waters, "What Are Justification and Sanctification?" *Tabletalk Magazine*

January 1, 2015 at https://www.ligonier.org/learn/articles/what-are-justification-and-sanctification/.

96   Ibid. Note that this last line describes what many refer to as the "Glorification" stage although Dr. Waters does not use that term here.

97   Council of Trent, "On Justification," First Decree, ch. X.

98   See the *Joint Declaration On The Doctrine Of Justification by the Lutheran World Federation and the Catholic Church* (vatican.va/roman_curia/pontifical_councils/chrstuni/documents/rc_pc_chrstuni_doc_31101999_cath-luth-joint-declaration_en.html).

99   Protestants have five doctrines that are qualified with the word *alone*: *sola scriptura* (Scripture alone), *sola fide* (faith alone), *sola gratia* (grace alone), *solo Christo* (Christ alone) and *soli Deo gloria* (to the glory of God alone). The key to understanding this odd-sounding collection is to realize that each one of these "solas" refers to a distinct position in Protestant theology, setting it off from something else. For example, "Scripture alone" sets off Sacred Scripture from Sacred Tradition. "Faith alone" sets off personal faith from good works. "Grace alone" is very close to "faith alone" but picks out the efficient cause of salvation (God's grace) from the instrumental cause (personal faith).

100   Faith, in the Free Grace system, is simply intellectual assent and does not require any special act of God: "'Intellectual assent' is a good definition of what faith is. For example, do you believe that George Washington was the first President of the United States? If you do, then you know what faith is from a biblical perspective. There is no commitment, no decision of the will, no turning from sins, and no works that are part of faith in Christ. If you are convinced or persuaded that what he promised is true, then you believe in him. Faith is passive." (Bob Wilkin, "What Is Free Grace Theology?" *Grace in Focus Articles* September 1, 2014 at https://faithalone.org/grace-in-focus-articles/what-is-free-grace-theology/).

101   This, I have found, is often the case with Protestant theology—and for good reason: its rejection of Catholicism usually entails affirming more extreme positions that favor only one portion of the same theological data the Church holds in balance. Whereas Catholic doctrine has been developing continuously since the beginning of the Church, building upon the conclusions and principles established by the apostles and their successors, Protestantism has had to create and then re-create itself every generation since the sixteenth century. This continual re-creation is not an accidental but an essential feature of Protestantism. They have a phrase to describe the process: *Semper Reformanda* (often translated as "reformed and always reforming").

102   See, for example, Thomas Aquinas, *Summa Theologiae* I Q. 19 and Q.23.

103   John D. Hannah, "Exodus," in *The Bible Knowledge Commentary: An Exposition of the Scriptures*, ed. J.F. Walvoord and R.B. Zuck, vol. 1 (Wheaton, IL: Victor Books, 1985), 135.

104   Norman L. Geisler and Thomas A. Howe, *When Critics Ask: A Popular Handbook on Bible Difficulties* (Wheaton, IL: Victor Books, 1992), 177.

105   Edwin A. Blum, "John," in *The Bible Knowledge Commentary: An Exposition of the Scriptures*, ed. J.F. Walvoord and R.B. Zuck, vol. 2 (Wheaton, IL: Victor Books, 1985), 318–319.

106   John D. Grassmick, "Mark," in *The Bible Knowledge Commentary: An Exposition of the Scriptures*, ed. J.F. Walvoord and R.B. Zuck, vol. 2 (Wheaton, IL: Victor Books, 1985), 112.

107   Evangelical scholar Stanley D. Toussaint shows the difficulty these stories pose to Evangelical theology when he adds what doesn't appear in the scriptural text of Acts 16: "Verse 31 is a key passage on the message of faith. All that is needed for justification is faith in the Lord Jesus. The jailer had asked what he should do. The answer was that

he need perform no works; he only needed to believe in Jesus who is the Lord. The words and your household mean those members of his house who were of sufficient age to believe would be saved (cf. v. 34) as they trusted Christ. Each member had to believe to be saved." Note that the passage does not say "he need perform no works," nor does it identify the members of his house as those "who were of sufficient age to believe," nor does it indicate that "each member had to believe to be saved." [Stanley D. Toussaint, "Acts," in *The Bible Knowledge Commentary: An Exposition of the Scriptures*, ed. J.F. Walvoord and R.B. Zuck, vol. 2 (Wheaton, IL: Victor Books, 1985), 400.]

108 Gabriel J. Fackre, ed. *What About Those Who Have Never Heard?: Three Views on the Destiny of the Unevangelized*, (Downers Grove, IL: IVP Academic, 1995).

109 This fact may be indirectly admitted in Eric Svendsen's book *Evangelical Answers: A Critique of Current Roman Catholic Apologists* (Lindenhurst, NY: Reformation Press, 1999). Although Svendsen's book claims to be a "critique of the major issues raised by Catholic apologists" (see "Introduction"), it does not have a single section devoted to salvation issues.

110 Though not all of them—in fact, non-Catholics from the original Reformer Martin Luther to Evangelical hero C.S. Lewis, from modern Baptist scholar Jerry Walls to Protestant theologian Roger Olson, affirm the possibility of a purgatorial state after death.

111 There are many examples of this: "Paul assures believers in 2 Corinthians 5:6–8 that to be 'away from the body' is to be 'at home with the Lord'" (C.A.R.M. http://carm. org/bible-about-purgatory). "For believers, after death is to be 'away from the body and at home with the Lord.' Notice that this does not say 'away from the body, in purgatory with the cleansing fire'" (Got Questions? www.gotquestions.org/purgatory. html). "The true intermediate state is found in 2 Corinthians 5:1–11. When we die as believers, we are immediately present with the Lord and absent from the body" (Ask the Pastors: askthepastors.wordpress.com/tag/purgatory/).

112 Evangelical scholar Ron Rhodes indirectly admits this in his book *Reasoning from the Scripture with Catholics* (Eugene, OR: Harvest House, 2000). Rhodes is forced to break 2 Corinthians 5:6–8 into separate pieces and then paraphrase it in order to make it appear that "it is the clear teaching of Scripture that, at the moment of death, believers go directly into the presence of God" (p. 239). Here is how he does it: "for believers 'to be absent from the body' is to be 'at home with the Lord'" (p. 240). Norman Geisler does a similar thing in his argument against purgatory by changing St. Paul's statement of hope into a declaration of certainty: "At death believers immediately 'leave the body and go home to the Lord' (2 Cor. 5:8)." Norman L. Geisler and Ralph E. MacKenzie, *Roman Catholics and Evangelicals: Agreements and Differences* (Grand Rapids, MI: Baker Books, 1995), 339.

113 For example, "Abraham's side" apparently refers to a place of paradise for Old Testament believers at the time of death (cf. Luke 23:43; 2 Cor. 12:3)" [John A. Martin, "Luke," in *The Bible Knowledge Commentary: An Exposition of the Scriptures*, ed. J.F. Walvoord and R.B. Zuck, vol. 2 (Wheaton, IL: Victor Books, 1985), 247]. The rich man went to Hades (v. 23). *Hades* is the Greek translation of the Hebrew word *sheol* and usually indicates the realm of the dead. Here it clearly refers to a place of torment. Possibly this parable is teaching that *sheol* is divided into two realms, one of blessing and one of punishment" [Thomas R. Schreiner, "Luke," in *Evangelical Commentary on the Bible*, vol. 3, Baker Reference Library (Grand Rapids, MI: Baker Book House, 1995), 829].

114 *Sheol*: 1 Samuel 2:6; Job 14:13; *Hades*: Luke 10:15, 16:23; *Abraham's Bosom*: Luke 16:22: *Paradise*: Luke 23:43. Importantly, St. John records that this realm of the dead still exists after Jesus' death and resurrection (Rev. 20:13–15).

115 The confidence Paul speaks of in 2 Corinthians 5:8 may only pertain to himself and others who demonstrate courage (v.6, 8), walk by faith (v. 7), and work to please God (v. 9), and do sufficient good works (v. 10). Thus, ironically, the need for purgatory may be implied by this passage!

116 Southerners might like to think of purgatory as heaven's "mudroom"—a place to get cleaned up before you go and track dirt all over the rest of the house!

117 Ron Rhodes, *Reasoning from the Scripture with Catholics* (Eugene, OR: Harvest House, 2000), 238.

118 "'Purification' or purging from our 'sins' was 'accomplished' (past tense) on the cross. Thank God that this is the only purgatory we will ever have to suffer for our sins. . . . all *experiential* sanctification occurs in this life before death (cf. 1 Cor. 3:10–13; 2 Cor. 5:10; Rev. 22:12). The only sanctification after death is *actual*. The Bible calls it glorification (Rom. 8:30; 1 John 3:2)." Norman L. Geisler and Ralph E. MacKenzie, *Roman Catholics and Evangelicals: Agreements and Differences* (Grand Rapids, MI: Baker Books, 1995), 338. Emphasis in original.

119 "We suffer trials so that our faith may be proved genuine (v. 7). . . . He [God] allows the trials to come so that the impurities of sin may be removed from us and so that our faith may become more precious. . . . that we may be found to praise, honor, and glory at the revelation of Jesus Christ" [Paul A. Cedar and Lloyd J. Ogilvie, James / 1 & 2 Peter / Jude, vol. 34, *The Preacher's Commentary Series* (Nashville, TN: Thomas Nelson Inc, 1984), 117]. "These various trials—which seem to refer to persecution rather than life's normal problems—have two results: (a) they refine or purify one's faith—much as gold is refined by fire when its dross is removed, and (b) trials prove the reality of one's faith" [Roger M. Raymer, "1 Peter," in *The Bible Knowledge Commentary: An Exposition of the Scriptures*, ed. J.F. Walvoord and R.B. Zuck, vol. 2 (Wheaton, IL: Victor Books, 1985), 841].

120 The oldest copies of the Hebrew scriptures (the Dead Sea Scrolls) and the earliest Old Testament translation (the Greek Septuagint) included these books and, interestingly, they were included in Protestant translations of the Bible (including the venerable King James Version) well into the nineteenth century. See Gary Michuta, *Why Catholic Bibles are Bigger* (Catholic Answers Press, 2017), 237–289.

121 Often stated as, "In essentials unity, in non-essentials liberty, and in all things charity," this phrase has often been assigned to St. Augustine or the Lutheran theologian Peter Meiderlin (Rupertus Meldeniu). However, it appears to come from a seventeenth-century writing from Marco Antonio de Dominis—an apostate Catholic who returned to the Church only to fall yet again and be declared a relapsed heretic by the Church!

122 Norman Geisler and Ron Rhodes, *Conviction Without Compromise: Standing Strong in the Core Beliefs of the Christian Faith* (Eugene, OR: Harvest House, 2008), 7. Note that this book's valiant effort to provide an objective basis for Christian unity ultimately failed. Indeed, it was based on Geisler's theory of essentials which he used to produce no fewer than three different "essentials" lists! See Douglas M. Beaumont, ed. *Evangelical Exodus: Evangelical Seminarians and Their Paths to Rome* (San Francisco, CA: Ignatius Press, 2016), Appendix 2.

123 "Letter XVII: Calvin To Cranmer, Archbishop Of Canterbury, Wishes Health" in Théodore de Bèze, *The Life of John Calvin*. Translated by Francis Sibson (Philadelphia, PA: Wm. S. Martin, Printer, 1836), 297–298.

ABOUT THE AUTHOR

Douglas M. Beaumont earned a Ph.D. in theology from North-West University and an M.A. in apologetics from Southern Evangelical Seminary, where he taught for many years before coming into full communion with the Catholic Church. He has since appeared on *The Journey Home, Catholic Answers Live,* and has been interviewed by *The National Catholic Register, EWTN,* and *Relevant Radio.* He is the author of *Evangelical Exodus* and *The Message Behind the Movie,* and has contributed to *Bumper Sticker Catholicism, The Best Catholic Writing, The Apologetics Study Bible for Students,* and the *Christian Apologetics Journal.* He can be found online at douglasbeaumont.com.